WRITING WITH STYLE

WRITING WITH STYLE

APA Style for Social Work

Fourth Edition

Lenore T. Szuchman
Barry University

Barbara Thomlison
Florida International University

BROOKS/COLE
CENGAGE Learning™

Australia • Brazil • Japan • Korea • Mexico • Singapore • Spain • United Kingdom • United States

BROOKS/COLE
CENGAGE Learning™

Writing With Style: APA Style for Social Work, **Fourth Edition**
Lenore T. Szuchman and Barbara Thomlison

Executive Editor:
Linda Schreiber-Ganster

Acquisitions Editor:
Seth Dobrin

Assistant Editor: Arwen Petty

Editorial Assistant:
Rachel McDonald

Media Editor: Dennis Fitzgerald

Marketing Manager:
Trent Whatcott

Marketing Assistant:
Darlene Macanan

Marketing Communications
Manager: Tami Strang

Content Project Management:
Pre-Press PMG

Creative Director: Rob Hugel

Art Director: Caryl Gorska

Print Buyer: Rebecca Cross

Production Service:
Pre-Press PMG

Copy Editor: Pre-Press PMG

Cover Designer: Jeremy Mende

Cover Image: I Dream Stock/
Masterfile

Compositor: Pre-Press PMG

For product information and technology assistance, contact us at **Cengage Learning Customer & Sales Support, 1-800-354-9706**

For permission to use material from this text or product, submit all requests online at **cengage.com/permissions** Further permissions questions can be emailed to **permissionrequest@cengage.com**

Library of Congress Control Number: 2009943795

ISBN-13: 978-0-8400-3198-3

ISBN-10: 0-8400-3198-X

Brooks/Cole
20 Davis Drive
Belmont, CA 94002-3098
USA

Cengage Learning is a leading provider of customized learning solutions with office locations around the globe, including Singapore, the United Kingdom, Australia, Mexico, Brazil, and Japan. Locate your local office at **www.cengage.com/global**

Cengage Learning products are represented in Canada by Nelson Education, Ltd.

To learn more about Brooks/Cole, visit
www.cengage.com/brookscole

Purchase any of our products at your local college store or at our preferred online store **www.CengageBrain.com**

Printed in the United States of America
1 2 3 4 5 6 7 13 12 11 10

Brief Contents

Table of Contents

Preface

We have designed *Writing With Style: APA Style for Social Work* with the single purpose of assisting students and beginning professionals with their writing. Good writing comes naturally for some people, but even for the experienced writer, it is hard work. For most people, writing is a difficult process. Having good ideas is only part of the writing process. The challenge comes in communicating those ideas clearly in writing, yet little time in social work education is devoted to improving writing skills. This book will help students develop the habits needed for proficient writing skills that lead to confidence for both the social work practice context and the academic context.

As a primer in the elements of APA style, this book should be used early in the student's social work education. However, students and professionals at any point in their social work education can benefit from the practical tips and guidelines contained in the book. We think *Writing With Style* will address writing issues in many settings: the classroom, the field, and conference presentations. We hope that it will make reading more enjoyable and using APA style guidelines less overwhelming and more understandable.

Goals of the Book

The primary goals of this book are to help students and professionals develop high-quality writing skills, whether their purpose is improving scholarly papers, or building skills for improving documentation of practice. Most social work students, whether at the undergraduate or graduate level, need to improve their writing skills, both for educational performance and for professional practice. The goals of this book are (1) to reduce confusion about writing in APA style, (2) to improve technical and scholarly writing skills in social work education and practice, and (3) to demonstrate the value and importance of developing writing skills. The goals are active and practical. This book provides the instruction, exercises, and structure needed for writing an effective paper. Once students master the basic elements of APA style, they will have the motivation and confidence to continue improving their writing.

Making Sense of APA Style Format

APA style writing is a skill that requires a substantial amount of practice. Social work students are usually expected to conform to APA guidelines in all their written work, including that assigned in research methods classes. Shortly after admission to the social work program, students must master a technical writing style that often contradicts what they learned in their first-year composition classes where the emphasis was on the Modern Language Association (MLA) style. In these courses, students generally learn how to organize a coherent paragraph, how to develop a thesis statement, and how to write an essay or a library research paper in the generic (MLA-based) style. This is a useful start, but it does not enhance students' technical writing skills when it comes to using APA guidelines. They must now learn to write using APA style, which includes not only rules made explicit in the *Publication Manual* but also other conventions that constitute the unwritten rules of APA style. For example, rather than writing about what other authors *said* or *believed,* students should concentrate on what the authors *found* or *reported.* Also, the title of an article should not be mentioned in a literature review, and passive voice may sometimes be used.

Using the Book

Similar to the previous editions, the fourth edition of this book continues the user friendly style with an emphasis on technical writing in an easy-to-understand presentation. After Chapter 1, which introduces the reasons that social work scholarship requires APA style, the *order of the chapters is flexible.* Chapter 2 discusses the ethics of writing, indicating the acceptable forms and practices of recognizing the ideas and intellectual property of others. Many writers assume they understand scholarly misconduct or plagiarism, but we strongly encourage all readers to consult this section before preparing any written assignments. Some will be surprised to learn that certain of their writing habits may qualify as scholarly misconduct or plagiarism and are unacceptable scholarly practices. After readers complete a few of the exercises, the concept of plagiarism should be clearer than before.

Chapter 3 contains general writing conventions, such as how to refer to the work of others in the body of a paper and tips for avoiding sexist language. It is general enough to be applicable to any section of a written paper or research report. Writing the specific sections of a paper is covered in Chapters 4 through 11 in the order in which many instructors teach them. But remember, they may be assigned in another order with no confusion for students. Chapter 3 contains guidance on avoiding the grammar and punctuation errors commonly found in social work papers. These include how to identify and avoid run-on sentences, how to use a colon, and how to apply rules accurately. These reflect the pet peeves of many professors. Students are encouraged to add notes on rules whose violations constitute the pet peeves of their own instructors. Chapter 6 presents guidance for writing a literature review. Literature reviews are a common assignment and necessary part of a research proposal or report. This chapter provides examples of outlines of writing in APA style, including a proposal and research report, a theoretical review paper, and the basic approach and summary of steps in conducting an Internet search for a literature review.

After writing the paper, Chapter 13 contains advice on rewriting. Beginning writers often assume that proofreading and revising are the same. We clarify the difference, and then make several specific suggestions for revising. Next, we lead readers through a series of proofreading exercises that direct them to rely on their word processors to spot areas of potential problems. We encourage readers to turn to these chapters early in the writing process. For those who are using this book for a course, for example, Chapters 3 and 13 can be consulted at any point in the development of an assigned paper. Therefore, it is not surprising that we recommend that students keep this book in their backpacks for easy access; are daily reasons for checking the tips we present, for all of writing projects.

The chapter on presentations, Chapter 14, is last because it provides readers with a real-world option for communicating scholarly views and findings. In fact, we think all students benefit from the experience of developing a presentation or the preparation for participating in case presentations, practice, and research conferences. Presentations teach social workers to integrate content and highlight key elements of a social work topic or research study, and for these reasons, it is important for students to practice this skill before graduation. We learned from previous editions that professionals using this book found this chapter very helpful because they often need to prepare poster presentations or oral presentations for conferences without having had any training for it in their degree programs.

We hope our ideas continue to be helpful, and we encourage readers to take many opportunities to present their work.

Social workers should not expect this book to replace the *Publication Manual*. They should be aware that this is one of several reference books that belong on their desk when they write. The exercises in *Writing With Style* do not cover every writing situation described in the *Publication Manual*. Instead, we provide general descriptions for writing social work research papers by condensing the most relevant material from the *Publication Manual* for writing review papers and research proposals, and we give primary emphasis to areas that social work students often find most difficult. Because almost everyone needs additional practice with certain basic grammar and punctuation rules, we also provide general rules throughout *Writing With Style*. We know that reviewing writing and making revisions improves the presentation of ideas, scholarly skills, and, we hope, grades.

We suggest using this book as an excellent companion for social work research, evaluation, and practice methods courses, including the integrative field education seminars. It is suitable in graduate and undergraduate programs. It is ideal for any course with writing requirements, for example, review articles, methodological papers, research proposals, oral presentations, and other writings. From this book, students can learn the proper APA format for those projects, including details such as writing titles, title pages, literature reviews, preparing tables, organizing references, and avoiding common writing errors. The exercises encourage active learning and reinforce the basic elements of writing with APA style that supplements any course work. Using this book may even assist students and professionals in less formal aspects of written work, such as documenting their practice, keeping journals, and writing case studies. With this book as a reference source for assignments and papers, social work students will be less intimidated by having to write papers using APA style. Practicing social workers can use this book to refresh these writing skills and learn about style standards that may have been revised since they graduated. Social work academics can use this book as a handy reference guide for manuscript preparation and grading of student assignments. The book's informal, easy-to-read style makes it suitable for a wide audience of people who need a quick reference to the basic and essential elements of writing with style using the APA guidelines.

Learning by Doing

Unlike the *Publication Manual,* this book is practical and active in its learning style. Readers will learn about scholarly writing through modeling the writing of published authors. This is a very effective approach. Completing the exercises in this book will familiarize readers with APA style by a method that also helps them begin to read APA publications. The exercises require students to scan APA publications for examples of particular rules and conventions. They then learn by modeling or practicing these techniques. They can use the lists they generate by completing the exercises in *Writing With Style* when they write your own papers—the words and phrases contained in the exercises exemplify not only APA style but also the social work scholar's style and form. Thus, readers benefit both from the *process of searching* for examples in social work journals and from the *item file* they develop for use in writing their own review articles, methods papers, and other written work.

It is daunting for the undergraduate social work student to see the *Publication Manual* and realize that all writing must conform to a style set out in what looks like a reference book rather than a style guide. In fact, the *Publication Manual* is both. And many students, even many professionals, need help in using it. For example, there are some rules in the *Publication Manual* that writers *must* learn, and there are others that they do not have to learn until these rules are relevant or needed for writing. That is, some rules must become second nature (e.g., the use of past tense for the research method of a study), and others are used only occasionally and do not have to be memorized (e.g., how to reference a court case). The exercises in this book focus on the rules that should be learned, while pointing to the types of things that should be looked up. We also call attention to the need for precision in word usage. Students who are new to scholarly writing have not always been trained to seek the type of precision required.

New in the Fourth Edition

We have kept this volume brief so that it can be used as a supplement for a variety of courses. For many courses, it is likely that students will have their own copies of the *Publication Manual* or the *Concise Rules,* but some instructors might find that there is enough material here for students to complete assignments for certain classes without purchasing either of these books. There are changes in this edition reflecting the most common changes in the *Publication Manual*. In brief, the changes included are as follows:

1. The most important change in this edition is that it is now based on style rules as expressed in the sixth edition of the *Publication Manual*. This includes, for example, updated material on the Participants section, and updates on avoiding bias in language. Furthermore, the tables at the end of each chapter are now keyed to that edition and to the current edition of the *Concise Rules* as well.

2. Some exercises are accompanied by reference to articles widely available online through university and college libraries. Many exercises have updated examples.

3. We have added some quick lists on the inside front and back covers. We hope these will be helpful for students as they begin to memorize rules that they will need to use often.

4. We have also moved the exercises from the end of the chapters so that they are now placed closer to the relevant material in each chapter.

5. In addition to these global changes, we have expanded sections on self-plagiarism, using "wiki" sources, referencing electronic sources, and creating tables and graphs, as well as thoroughly revising the section on preparing poster presentations with attention to PowerPoint formatting.

The topics are keyed to the relevant section and subsection of the *Publication Manual* and *Concise Rules* to be helpful for all writing projects. However, we urge students to keep *Writing With Style* as a prominent book at hand for all your social work writing now and in the future. Finally, we have made a minor change by reducing the number of examples that the students have to find for many of the exercises.

Acknowledgments

Again, we would like to acknowledge the many people whose observations, suggestions, and advice assisted us in the preparation of the first edition. We continued to get good advice from many people in succeeding editions, and now, for the fourth editions, we wish to thank the following reviewers: Beth Walker of WNMU; Marina Lalayants of Hunter College, CUNY; Robert J. Wolf of Eastern Connecticut State University; Amanda Haboush of University of Nevada Las Vegas; Susan Tebb of Saint Louis University; Leon Battista of Bronx Community College; Dr. Lisa E. Cox of The Richard Stockton College of New Jersey; Thomas McMillian of Shaw University; Butler-Jones of Elms College; Louise Walton of Northeastern State University; Dr. Michael Cronin of Richard Stockton College of NJ; Renee Askew of Shaw University; Bethany Lighthart of Southwestern Michigan College; Jeff Wylie of Murray State University; and Curtis Proctor of Wichita State University. We'd also like to thank Pre-Press PMG for making the production phase so seamless.

Special thanks are due to the many students and colleagues who have taken the time to communicate to us just how helpful the book was in their social work and education courses.

We are indebted always to Lisa Gebo, who was Executive Editor at Brooks/Cole Wadsworth Publishing, for her effervescent encouragement and support. Lisa introduced the two of us, and we are thankful for the productive relationship that has ensued. Also we thank Seth Dobrin and his staff for their suggestions and assistance to this revised edition. Finally, we would like to thank our own families, who have been supportive and passionate advocates of our work.

Lenore T. Szuchman
LSzuchman@mail.barry.edu
Barbara Thomlison
Barbara.Thomlison@fiu.edu

WRITING WITH STYLE

1
Writing With Style

As authors, we begin by emphasizing that this is not a typical book about writing. This book originally was written as an active learning guide to help beginning students and scholars of social work to develop and practice the skills needed to write using APA style and format. The fourth edition has the same overall purpose, but the focus has expanded to consider the needs of many experienced social workers and faculty members who have found the book immensely instructive and handy for use in preparation of manuscripts for professional journals. In other words, this book is designed to help you with all kinds of writing assignments and requirements you may face on a daily basis as a professional or an about-to-be social worker.

You are probably wondering why it is important to pay attention to the content, style and format of your writing. For a professional social worker, it is not acceptable to write as a lay person. Acquiring knowledge about the helping process and working with people and their environments both involve not only communicating verbally but also in writing. Learning to practice as a professional requires writing as a professional social worker, which is easier said than done. In addition to writing in order to document observations, practitioners increasingly are called upon to write articles for publication, research proposals, and presentations for training sessions or conferences and workshops. Your purpose for writing may be to improve your written assignments; to summarize evidence-based research studies, literature reviews, case studies, and reports; or to prepare manuscripts for publication. Writing for professional purposes requires that you pay attention to elements of style or format that you may not have considered relevant in the past. Given the wide professional purposes you may encounter, this book is designed to help you write in the appropriate style, as a step on your way to becoming a professional social worker.

The Stylistic Distinction for Scientific Journals

The scholarly articles in social work journals are different in style and presentation from the popular psychology books on human behavior found on the shelves of your local bookstore. The best of those books translate the findings of research on human behavior into language that makes the information easy for the nonscientific reader to access and apply. By contrast, you are expected to write your papers in an entirely different fashion. If you are now enrolled in a social work program, you have, to some extent, already moved beyond the point of reading the self-help and popular psychology books (although they may continue to provide enjoyment for you). You are reading the scholarly journals read by professional social workers and preparing written assignments for your professor; you may be documenting case assessments and plans during an internship for your field instructor. Your instructor will expect your writing to reflect the scientific approach and scholarly quality of the journal articles you are reading. If you are a professional using this book to enhance your skills, then you certainly know how important professional writing style can be.

Professionals read various scholarly materials with attention to different levels of detail. Not all professionals read with the same focus. The reader who is highly expert in a certain area of research or practice might be most interested in the Literature Review, Design, Method, or Implications section of an article. The person who skims needs to be able to predict where the hypotheses will be and where the most important outcome will be. Finally, a student or researcher studying a particular area needs to check the reference list to see what further reading might be warranted.

You can see that if all parts of an article are written in a standardized way, each reader's needs can be met efficiently. For the sake of clarity, this kind of writing can get repetitive, but it can still be interesting to read, and in the best examples, the prose is fluid and elegant. Certainly, one hopes that the research findings alone generate excitement in at least a few readers. However, there can be no suspense, no teasing about the problems or their solutions, no surprise endings. If generating suspense were important, the first thing to do would be to eliminate the abstract. Even topic sentences for paragraphs detract from suspense. And if thrills were important, results that support the hypotheses would be listed first, instead of in the order in which the hypotheses were originally presented. Surprise endings?

Not for professionals. They decide whether to read a research article or report only after knowing how the study came out.

Okay, you are probably ready to agree that professionals need a prose style different from that required by the general public. But why do different professionals need different rules? Why can't everyone use Modern Language Association (MLA) or *The Chicago Manual of Style* rules? One reason is that different professions rely on different methods and different styles of argument. Social workers and psychologists need a format different from that of historians or literary critics. They have their own type of information to convey and their own values as consumers of their own literature. The National Association of Social Workers (NASW) and other social work organizations publish information within their professional community through an increasing number of scholarly journals. The numerous journals devoted to social work, social welfare, social work research, evidence-based practice, and the social work community reflect a trend to publishing specializations in social work education, practice, and research (Mendelsohn, 1997; Thyer, 1994). The editors of these journals consider thousands of submissions each year. The rules set forth in the *Publication Manual of the American Psychological Association,* sixth edition (2010), facilitate the handling of such a large number of manuscripts by standardizing much of the format. These rules have been so convenient for readers and writers that many other science and social science journals adhere to a similar framework.

You will certainly want to own the *Publication Manual* or the *Concise Rules of APA Style,* sixth edition (American Psychological Association, 2010), and use one of them as a reference. But a reference book is just that—something you refer to when you are not sure of a rule. You are not expected to learn all the rules. No social worker submits a manuscript without having to look up some rules in the *Publication Manual* along the way. Why memorize the citation format for reviews of videos or for a non-English chapter in an edited book? Look it up—we all do.

Some conventions, however, need to be learned because you use them so often. Some are style rules you have encountered elsewhere, such as rules about agreement of subject and verb and when to use *between* versus *among,* and it is time you master these rules. Other conventions are unique to the social sciences, for example, using past tense for the results and present tense for the conclusions, abbreviating more liberally in the abstract than in the body of the paper, and using metric units whenever possible.

Unfortunately, there is more to sounding like a social worker than following all the style rules—just as there is more to sounding like a Texan than speaking English. If you want to sound like a Texan, you have to listen to a lot of Texans talk. If you want to write like a social worker, you have to read a lot of literature in social work and related disciplines. But even though it seems illogical, you must begin to learn how to write like a social worker even before you have the opportunity to read a great deal of professional literature in the field.

Why Practitioners Need to Read Research Articles

As a student moving toward a professional social work career it is necessary for you to graduate with the tools to have a successful, rewarding, and enjoyable career. To reach this goal, you need to read professional or scientific journals to acquire both the practical information and theoretical foundation needed to be successful. To provide effective interventions for clients, you need to read about evidence-based treatments, and this requires that you read about the processes and approaches to using the best research for practice. With that in mind, why should you engage in reading empirical studies, literature reviews, theoretical articles, and case studies? There are several compelling reasons. First, access to research articles is currently considered essential information for delivering best practices to client groups. Professionals involved in complex and challenging issues need access to approaches that support sound decisions. These decisions are based on the best available published information. Second, in the years after you graduate, keeping your knowledge and skills up to date is important and necessary. You need to stay on top of new developments, new interventions, and practice frameworks as they occur, while at the same time getting accustomed to a new job, new colleagues, and possibly even a new location for that first job. Thus, keeping abreast is very challenging and knowing how to access research articles and reading about these findings is essential. It is not your job to know everything, even in your area of expertise, but it is your job to be able to find the information and read about it when you and your clients need it. Finally, it is an issue of ethics and accountability to engage in competent practice. Reading research is one approach to doing this. This book emphasizes the importance of continuing to read and write after graduation. Now let's talk about how to start writing and using what you discovered from your reading.

Getting Started

This book is a reference for writing in APA style. It is both a rule book and a workbook. It is designed to prepare you to write your first social work paper or research report or to help you improve your writing after receiving disappointing grades on previous assignments. It will guide you through the social work literature in a way that will focus your attention on how authors use words and phrases. It will teach you to keep lists of examples of these words and phrases so that when you write papers, you can refer to your lists for models to help you construct sentences and paragraphs of your own. This book does *not* replace the *Publication Manual* or the *Concise Rules of APA Style*. When you write papers, you should keep one of those reference books and this filled-in workbook near you. This book is your *sample* book. If you want to produce a sentence or phrase in the way a more experienced writer of social work articles would, use your lists developed from these exercises. If you want to find out exactly how to organize, abbreviate, or punctuate a technical section, sentence, or phrase, use the *Publication Manual* or the *Concise Rules of APA Style*. By the way, when you use the *Publication Manual,* you may worry that it sometimes seems to contradict the printed format of the journals themselves. That is because your papers are *manuscripts,* and manuscripts differ from printed material. Your responsibilities are those of the author of a manuscript, not those of a printer preparing pages for a journal.

You will find two types of exercises in this book. The first and most frequently presented will result in the lists of usable sentences and phrases described above. To produce these lists, use sentence frames; that is, leave blanks for the words that are specific to the research being presented. For example, suppose you find the following sentence in a journal and it is an example of what you are looking for: "These findings regarding writing social work outcomes have several implications." Substitute a blank space when you copy it for your list of examples: "These findings regarding ___ have several implications." In most of the exercises, we have sampled several journals and filled in the first few items for you with frames from our own search. Sometimes we have filled in the blanks for fun. Feel free to do the same with your own examples.

The second type of exercise is designed to help you understand a point of grammar by finding examples of it. These exercises are found in Chapter 4, "Grammar and Punctuation Matters." Doing the exercises should help you learn the rules so that you never have to look them up again.

If you are using this book in a class, your instructor will guide you to the journals you should be looking at to do the various exercises. Otherwise, social work journals using APA format are suitable. However, you should be aware that whereas many journals are oriented to a specialized social work content or theoretical focus (e.g., *Journal of Public Child Welfare, Clinical Social Work Journal, Social Work, Social Service Review, Affilia: The Journal of Women and Social Work, International Social Work, Human Services in the Rural Environment, Canadian Social Work Review, Administration in Social Work*), others accept an eclectic range of articles (e.g., *Journal of Family Issues, Journal of Gerontological Social Work, Journal of Evidence-Based Social Work, Journal of Forensic Social Work*). Some publish the results of scholarly enquiry, notably, *Research on Social Work Practice, Children and Youth Services Review,* and *Social Work Research,* and still other journals specialize in review articles (e.g., *Journal of Clinical Psychology Review; Trauma, Violence, & Abuse*). Unless otherwise noted, the assignments in this book require that you look at empirical (research), conceptual (model building, theory development, interdisciplinary explorations), or descriptive (accounts of populations, programs, services) articles. You can find out whether APA guidelines are followed by a journal in a section called "Instructions to Authors" printed in any current edition of that journal.

If you are not being directed to specific journals to use, our advice is to sample from a variety of sources. Go to a computerized database or to the library's current periodicals area and find a single issue of any of the following journals:

American Journal on Addictions

Behavior Therapy

Brief Treatment and Crisis Intervention

Child Abuse & Neglect: The International Journal

Child and Family Social Work

Child Maltreatment

Child Welfare

Families in Society

Human Services in the Rural Environment

Journal of Evidence-Based Social Work

Journal of Health & Social Policy

Journal of Human Behavior and the Social Environment

Journal of Public Child Welfare

Journal of Research on Adolescence

Research on Social Work Practice

Social Service Review

Social Work

Social Work Research

The Gerontologist

Why Are We Not Using APA Style in this Book?

We want to draw your attention to our style in this book. In preparing this book, we have intentionally used an informal style and tone to communicate to you, which does not strictly adhere to APA format. However, the rules and guidelines we present are about APA style and format; also the exercises are written in APA style. We have chosen a light, informal, and amusing style to make this content easier to read and remember; therefore, it differs from the *Publication Manual* which is a reference book. In fact, the journal articles you will read are designed to inform, not to amuse. They do not contain informal language, slang, contractions, or humor, and they do not address the reader as "you." If we were to write this book in that formal tone, it would be a good example for you, but it would not serve our purpose. Undoubtedly, you write in different ways for different purposes already. Now that you are learning the basic rules of a scientific style for a new purpose, we do not want you to model your scientific prose on novels, newspapers, or textbooks—or any sources other than those specifically written in APA style. But textbooks do not necessarily benefit from such a style. Therefore, we have chosen not to conform strictly to APA tone in this book. However, we hope that you will not catch us making spelling, grammar, or punctuation errors.

2

Ethics and Writing

Creating an ethically sound, well-written paper requires attention to many elements of your writing. Essentially, it requires principled commitment to the intrinsic values of science, as well as attention to the values of honesty, integrity, and legalities of ethics and writing. These are principles that need thoughtful consideration at the beginning of your writing, not at the end. When attended to, they bring the joy and feeling of pride in a well-written paper that follow hard work and independent research. Students often think they are aware of these rules concerning what is considered unethical or may constitute plagiarism. However, by reviewing the ethics of using sources before starting to write you may avoid unintentional problems. These problems, in fact, can result in serious consequences, penalties, and often the involvement of other authors, and even publishers, because it is assumed that ignorance is no excuse. Based on our experience, we find that students are often surprised to learn of the variety of behaviors that contribute to integrity (or lack of it) in scholarly writing. As professors, we have learned that many students are still uncertain about what constitutes ethical writing even after several years in secondary school and college. The key rules are presented in this chapter, but following are several sources that may be helpful if you need a broader view about ethics in writing or if you are unsure about the use of citing information in your papers. They will also be useful in handling and documenting confidential information for your internship:

■ Review the NASW *Code of Ethics* (National Association of Social Workers, 2008s). For a copy of the Code of Ethics, go to the NASW website: http://www.socialworkers.org/pubs/code/default.asp Section 4, particularly subsections 4.04 and 4.08, which discuss dishonesty, fraud, deception, and acknowledging sources.

◼ Consult the *Publication Manual of the American Psychological Association*, sixth edition (2010, pp. 11–20).

◼ Check your university, college, or school's policy and guidelines on plagiarism, academic conduct, or academic integrity which are usually found in the student handbook, and probably on a website as well.

Your profession places high value on ethical conduct in practice with clients, and this also includes ethical conduct in learning and writing about social work practice. When you submit a written assignment with your name on it, you are claiming everything in that work as yours unless you stipulate otherwise. One of the most common and important categories of misconduct in scholarly writing is *plagiarism*. Simply stated, plagiarism is taking or passing off ideas and writings from others as one's own. This includes using information and ideas from any published or unpublished source, including books, chapters, articles, and manuals, as well as information from the Internet. Plagiarism can be thought of as literary theft and is concerned with more than just using someone else's words. "Sometimes this is done unintentionally because of poor work habits; sometimes it is deliberate. In either case it is plagiarism and unacceptable" (Stefani & Carroll, 2001, p. 4).

There are two excellent reasons not to plagiarize. First, plagiarism is a form of cheating, and it is wrong (i.e., fraudulent) and therefore violates your internalized code of personal, academic, and professional ethics. Second, it also violates external codes of ethics, and that can have various consequences, none of them pleasant (Rothery, 2006). It is not known exactly how much of the plagiarism found in students' work is unintentional. But whether the behavior is intentional or unintentional, the penalties may be severe and are certainly disagreeable. The cost in terms of time and emotional strain can be enormous. Preventive measures need to be taken. It is a writer's responsibility to cite a source correctly both when a work is quoted directly and when it is reconfigured. Reconfiguring an author's work may entail paraphrasing, summarizing, and modifying content and ideas. Finally, checking with the instructor is the best strategy for a student who remains confused and unclear about what constitutes plagiarism.

Thus, with plagiarism as with criminal law, lack of knowledge or ignorance is no excuse. Finding out about all forms of plagiarism before writing is the best form of prevention. By working through this book, you have committed yourself to the effort of sharpening your writing skills. Therefore, it is also a good time to consider the variety of misdeeds that you might accidentally commit when preparing your written scholarly work so that you can avoid them.

Using Exact Words and Sentence Structure

Everyone seems to know that using someone else's words without giving that author credit is unacceptable. This rule is quite simple to follow: Use quotation marks (or a block quote form) when you are using someone's exact words and indicate specifically where the original is to be found, including the page number. Failing to do this is plagiarism even if you attribute the ideas to the proper person, because in that case, you have made it seem as if the ideas may have been borrowed but the words are your own. For example, suppose you are writing a paper on narrative theory applied to social work practice, and you are struck by the profundity and incisiveness of the following:

> There is always an unequal distribution of power in the therapeutic context, regardless of the steps that are taken by therapists to render the content of therapy more egalitarian. And as previously discussed, the potential for this unequal distribution of power to be disqualifying and objectifying of people is greater in team contexts. In view of this, it is important that steps be taken to counter possible toxic effects of this power imbalance, to reduce the potential for harm. One contribution to such steps is for reflecting team members to assist each other to deconstruct their responses. This can be achieved if team members invite each other to embody their comments with, or situate their speech acts in, the history of their personal experience, interests, intentions, imagination, and so on. If reflecting team members take responsibility to deconstruct their comments and questions in this way, this does provide at least some safeguard against the sort of imposition of "truth" that is the outcome of disembodied speech acts (White, 1995, pp. 187–188).

If you take any part of this passage and place it verbatim (word for word) in work of which you are the declared author, that is plagiarism. Michael White does not own the individual words he has used to compose this paragraph, but the patterning and purpose of the words are his intellectual property. If you use so much as a brief phrase from his work in yours, make sure it is clear that you are quoting, and give him credit (Rothery, 2006).

Changing Words and Sentence Structure

Using the ideas of another author but not the exact words also requires a reference to the source. For example, suppose you want to present the information in the following quote in your work, but you feel that it would fit better if written differently.

> Of course, the relationship between clinical social workers and their clients is never truly equal, no matter how one tries to achieve this—and the imbalance is especially pronounced when a team of workers is part of the therapeutic effort. (White, 1995)

Often, students would like to paraphrase ideas and give credit for them, but they cannot think of original ways to say them. Paraphrasing is a skill that takes some effort to acquire, so it is not surprising that when students find a useful thought in someone else's writing they are stymied about how a paraphrase can ever be better than the original. Some turn to the thesaurus to solve the problem. They leave the sentence more or less the way the author wrote it but use a thesaurus to find words that might replace some of the original words. These students assume that once they change a few words in another person's work, the sentence no longer requires quotation marks and can legitimately be claimed as their own. If the following sentence is presented with no citation, though, it will still qualify as plagiarism even though some changes have been made:

> Regardless of the steps that are taken by therapists to be egalitarian, there is always an unequal distribution of power in the consulting room.

The writer is representing what is still White's work (crosscheck it against the first sentence in the main quote) as her or his own, and a reader who assumes that this sentence originated with someone other than White will be deceived.

Suppose you are a clear thinker and decide that you should rewrite Michael White's work in plain English. This is always a challenge with postmodernist writers, but it is early in the term, and you have not lost your energy and ambition yet. After considerable effort, you render White's passage as follows:

> It is difficult for social workers and clients to have a truly equal relationship, especially when teams are used and the client has several workers to contend with. This can be damaging to clients if they feel that they have too little power or are being treated like a "case" rather than a real person. One solution to this problem is for team members to self-disclose about experiences of their own that are relevant to the client's situation. When team members are personally open in this way, clients are less likely to feel dehumanized and disrespected.

This may have undergone enough reworking that shared credit for the outcome is appropriate, but it is still best to indicate that White got the writer started on the paragraph (despite the fact that it is considerably improved). There are different ways of accomplishing this:

> *To paraphrase White (1995),* it is seldom, if ever, possible for . . .

> *As White (1995) and others have pointed out in their discussions of the helping relationship,* it is difficult for . . .

> *When team members are personally open in this way, clients are less likely to feel disrespected (White, 1995).* (Rothery, 2006)

There is a way to be fairly safe from unintentional plagiarism. Never try to paraphrase one sentence at a time. Instead, first read through the whole section you wish to paraphrase, then write your paraphrase but without looking at the original. Then, be sure to credit the ideas conveyed in the paraphrased sections to their author. If you must quote a phrase or a sentence, do so, using quotation marks for the quoted materials. But don't try to change the original just a bit and think it is a paraphrase.

Changing the Format

Now that you have learned to avoid violating someone's sentence structure, what about the structure of a larger unit? Suppose you find a literature review on the same subject as your own? What is the plagiarism risk in this case? If you organize the material around the same themes, you have plagiarized. If you use the same examples to make the same point, you have plagiarized. To prevent these forms of plagiarism, consider using the reference list of the literature review to help you with your library work, but don't read the actual review article until you have drawn some conclusions of your own. Then when you find that the review author has made a point you would like to add to your review, you can cite that author for having had a certain insight about some research that you have also read but from which you did not gain the same insight. You can even cite the author of the literature review for finding themes in the literature that organized the topic in a useful way.

Borrowing and Recycling Ideas

What about borrowing ideas from your professor or your textbook? To be safe, you must give credit in those cases as well. You may well be expected to get your knowledge from these sources, but if you use that knowledge in a written product of your own, cite the sources.

Self-plagiarism is the reuse of your own words and ideas, taking them from one paper and using them in another paper as if this were the first time you used them. It is also unethical to use your own words for more than one paper as if you had written them afresh for each class.

> If you prepared an assignment for one class and resubmit it for another, this is *deceptive*. Even if you do more work on it in the form of additions and revisions, it is deceptive to submit it as if it was prepared primarily for the assignment in question. There are grey areas—the work you do for one [written assignment] can legitimately build on work you have done for another. In these cases, it is your responsibility to check with the instructor, clarifying your plans and obtaining agreement with them. (Rothery, 2006)

Each professor expects that work written to fulfill the requirements of a certain class will be submitted only for that class. After all, researchers are not permitted to publish the same paper in two journals. And no one is allowed to sell a product as new if it has been used previously. If you have a paper already written that seems to serve the needs of another assignment, check with the second professor for guidance about how much of the paper needs to be refreshed before you recycle it for the second class. In general, the parts of the paper cannot be reused or reworked as an original piece of work.

Students sometimes have difficulty deciding when a statement needs a reference and when a point of view is their own. You do not need to cite someone else for your own opinions or for generally agreed-upon facts or principles. Your own opinion is easy to identify. For example, you may say:

> Our practice experiences differ from the research findings of the Greenspan (1998) study. In many cases, children as well as other family members often desire ongoing contact with parents, siblings, and other relatives even though a permanent return home is not possible. Consequently, we suggest caution is needed in adopting the findings from the Greenspan study if working with seriously emotionally disturbed children.

By contrast, at least in social work, it is difficult to decide which facts are generally agreed upon. It is tempting to assume that everyone sees behavior exactly as you do. For example, most observers may agree that adolescence is a time when self-esteem is fragile. But wait. Are you as sure about that as you are about the fact that in the United States, adolescents are expected to attend school? In fact, when you talk about psychological constructs such as self-esteem, you are very near the divide between fact and nonfact. If you cannot find a reference for your assertion about self-esteem, at least qualify it somewhat. Perhaps you can assert that there *seems* to be an emphasis in our culture on the fragility of adolescent self-esteem. If you have searched the literature on self-esteem, then you will have references at your disposal to cite when you make an assertion. Cite them, and you are safe.

Technical Phrases and Attribution

Students who are new to a field may also be confused about when a phrase is a standard technical term and when it is an original term. You are free to use technical phrases without attribution. Usually, it is safe to use effects that authors study (e.g., transfer of training) or variables they use (e.g., attitudes toward help-seeking) without quotation marks. If you are not sure if a short phrase you are using should be attributed to an author, use no quotation marks, but do include a page reference along with the rest of the citation information.

You may have begun to wonder why you will be safe from committing plagiarism by using this workbook as intended: copying sentences from published sources into this book and then using those very sentences later in your own papers. The reason you can do that is the same reason you can use a dictionary or a book of foreign phrases without fear of plagiarism. You need to learn how words are used before you can use them on your own. People who share a subculture, as do scholars in any discipline, tend to use words and even whole phrases in a particular way. As you do the exercises in this book, you will find that the same phrases keep appearing in the articles you scan. You may even have difficulty finding enough different examples of a given type to fill the spaces provided. As rich as the English language is, only a finite number of ways exist for phrasing a prediction or the results of a *t* test. When a form is used repeatedly, you are allowed to use it without fear that someone else "owns" it.

The Internet

The Internet has made plagiarism much easier. You can cut and paste whole sections of someone else's work into your own (not that you would!) without even transcribing it. *The New York Times* (Rimer, 2003, September 3) reported on a study by Donald McCabe, a professor at Rutgers University, who found that 38% of undergraduate students said that in the last year, they had done just that: cut and pasted from the Internet without citing the source. Nearly half of these students did not think that they had cheated. Perhaps this practice is made more appealing because much of what students find on the Internet does not seem to have an author or a date of publication. That does not mean, however, that stealing it is legal. It may mean that it has little intellectual value, and students should always be wary of using unsigned sources. But the *APA Manual* has gone to great lengths to establish formats for Internet citation. "In general, we recommend that you include the same elements, in the same order, as you would for a reference to a fixed-media source and add as much electronic retrieval information as needed for others to locate the sources you cited" (p. 187). We'll get back to this in greater detail in Chapter 11, "Listing References."

One problem even for honest folks is that many websites do not have authors or dates of publication. That seems to make it both difficult to cite and tempting to believe that the material is not "owned" so that using it is not stealing. Well, it is owned—even if the identity of the writer is not obvious.

In general, do not cut and paste from these sources. Print the whole website if your custom is to photocopy articles for your papers. Take notes from the screen if your habit is to do that in the library (rather than photocopying). A good guideline is to "use a little and give credit" (Talab, 2000, p. 7). In fact, that is just about the same advice we could give for print sources as well. Once you have used a little from a lot of sources, you have transformed the material into something of your own, and you have broken no laws.

3

General Writing Techniques

Even though social workers are concerned primarily with how they can help clients, it is striking that one of the most common topics they actually write about is each other. The fact is that a great part of scholarly writing about social work concerns the work previously done by other scholars in the discipline. The longest part of a published research study is often the introduction, in which the author surveys the research that led to the current study. Advanced students and researchers often write research proposals that emphasize the same type of material found in the introductions of printed articles. Finally, students are often assigned to write literature reviews as term papers. Therefore, it is very important to learn what the *Publication Manual* has to say about referring to and conveying the ideas and findings of other authors. Likewise, it is valuable to search some journals to see what generalizations can be made about unwritten rules.

Referring to Other Authors

When you refer to the work of another author or authors, use last names only and do not mention the titles of their works. Always name the author or authors of the chapter you have read in an edited book, not the editor of the book. The publication year is a necessary part of the citation, but it is seldom presented as part of the sentence. Students often write, "In 1995, Thomlison did a study of . . ." However, it is much more appropriate to keep the year in parentheses unless you are making a special point of the date. When you refer to the same study twice within a single paragraph, include the year in only the first instance.

19

Refer to other authors by last name only and do not mention the titles of their work (except in the References section).

You have the option of inserting the author's name and year of publication in parentheses: "A study of children who received treatment foster care interventions revealed that they are more likely to return to less restrictive environments than children receiving group care interventions (Thomlison, 2002)." If you do this, however, do not also include the author in the body of the same sentence. An example of this type of *error* is the following sentence: "Thomlison's study of children in treatment foster care has revealed they are more likely to return to less restrictive environments than children receiving group care (Thomlison, 2002)."

Another problem with regard to citations is how to refer to works that you have not read. First, try to get every relevant article and read it. However, you may cite material from secondary sources when you have not read the originals. Be aware that this does not allow you to put the sources you have not read yourself (primary sources) on your reference list. Put the source you *read* in the References section. In the body of the paper, you can mention the original work and indicate that you found mention of it in a secondary source—which you do cite: "Corcoran (as cited in Szuchman & Thomlison, 2009) found evidence that planned and systematic efforts to produce change in clients resulted in increased positive outcomes compared to unplanned and inconsistent efforts." Szuchman and Thomlison will be on your reference list; Corcoran will not. See page 13 in Chapter 2 of this book for an example in which we cite Rothery, who cites White. Now look in our reference list at the end of this book and see which of these two authors is listed.

If you have not read a source, do not list it in your References section. In the body of the paper, refer to the source you did read (secondary source) and indicate that the primary source was cited in the secondary source.

A potential source of confusion exists when someone else's research is referred to as the "current" study, the "present" study, or "this" study. These terms always refer to the study reported in the Method and Results sections of the article you are reading (or the research report you are writing). When you are looking at an article and writing about the outcome of that author's study in your own paper, you may come across these phrases, and they may find their way into your description of that study. Do not allow this. You may confuse your readers even more than this paragraph has confused you! And for the same reason.

Do not use "the current study" or "the present study" to refer to someone else's work.

One feature of our profession is that social workers are very polite when disagreeing with colleagues or disapproving of their work. You should be sensitive to this tone in your own reviews of the literature. A social worker who feels that Simpson has done a terrible study may only say, "Other researchers have failed to replicate Simpson's result" or "Simpson may have failed to take into account the . . ." Be careful about your tone when describing a controversial issue. Present both sides and indicate what kind of data support one conclusion and what kind support the other.

Words and Phrases to Collect

The English language contains so many words and expressions that it may come as a surprise to know how often social workers use the same ones over and over again. This is actually of benefit to the new writer, because with a collection of stock words and phrases, anyone can *sound* like a social worker, even while still learning to *think* like one. In this section, you will create a collection of some of these words and phrases to sprinkle into your own writing. First, consider how often sentences in a literature review are constructed around a researcher or a research study as the grammatical subject, for example, "Fraser and Thyer (1991) demonstrated that . . ." You may be tempted to vary your sentences by choosing the author as the grammatical subject sometimes and the research study at other times. Be cautious about this. You are obligated to use verbs that logically suit the abilities of your grammatical subjects. People are capable of many activities (verbs), but studies can *do* hardly anything. Consider this problem whenever you are tempted to begin a sentence with "The study . . ." Exactly what can a study do?

At least one example for every exercise in this chapter can be found in this article:

Judge, T. A., Hurst, C., & Simon, L.S. (2009). Does it pay to be smart, attractive, or confident (or all three)? Relationships among general mental ability, physical attractiveness, core self-evaluations, and income. *Journal of Applied Psychology, 94,* 742–755.

You should find articles yourself to fill in the remaining blanks.

 # Exercise 1

Select several articles that cover topics of interest to you or that have been assigned in your course. Find verbs in which the grammatical subject of a sentence is someone's *study, work, experiment,* or *research.* It may also be useful to include the object of that verb.

1. employs methods

2. demonstrates

3. provides evidence

4. _____

5. _____

6. _____

Another nonhuman grammatical subject that is often found in research reports is the outcome of someone's research. The words to look for here are *findings, results,* and *evidence.* Do not be surprised if the list you create for this exercise has a lot of overlap with the previous one.

 **Exercise 2**

List the verbs in sentences in which the subject is some kind of experimental *outcome*.

1. demonstrates

2. can be explained

3. suggests

4. _____

5. _____

6. _____

What can theories do? What can be done to them?

 **Exercise 3**

Find the verbs or verb phrases that are used with *theories* or *hypotheses*.

1. take something as evidence

2. have been challenged

3. focus on

4. lead to the hypothesis that

5. _____

6. _____

7. _____

You may have noticed in completing the previous three exercises that authors often use passive verb constructions when discussing a study, an outcome, or a theory. For example, they will note that a study *was designed* for some purpose. That type of writing shows you that the author knows that studies themselves cannot assess or find or test. Authors design studies so that they (the authors) can assess things. In contrast to inanimate studies and abstractions such as theories, a researcher or group of researchers can very easily be the grammatical subject of a sentence. In this case, look for sentences in which the subject is a specific author or authors or a more general noun such as *author, researcher,* or *experimenter.*

 # Exercise 4

List the verbs associated with *researchers.* (Here, you have been given plenty of space for a long list.) When you find a word more than once, put a check mark next to it every time you find it.

1. have shown

2. found

3. replicated

4. reported

5. _____

6. _____

7. _____

8. _____

9. _____

10. _____

11. _____

12. _____

13. _____

14. _____

15. _____

16. _____

17. _____

18. _____

_Use a person (e.g., "the researcher" or a proper name)
rather than a product (e.g., a study or a finding) as a
sentence subject whenever possible._

Now that you know 15 things that social workers _do_, please take note of the words you did _not_ find. You probably did not find _feel_. Research studies cannot feel, and researchers keep their feelings to themselves. Also, you found less _thinking_ and _believing_ than you might have expected. Perhaps _believe_ doesn't convey the scientific attitude as well as _hypothesize_ does. Likewise, researchers very often _reason_, but it seems as if they hardly ever _think_. Another group of words that will be rare in your lists is related to writing and talking: _stated, wrote, said_. Journalists and literary critics are interested in what people say and write. Social workers refer to the writings of others to report what they found or investigated.

_Do not indicate what researchers thought, felt, believed,
or said._

Another type of verb that social workers use can be categorized as a "hedge word." We hedge even when we hold strong opinions about why people behave as they do, because usually we cannot be absolutely sure of cause and effect. Even the most carefully designed studies do not provide ironclad evidence that allows us to generalize with absolute certainty about behavior. Therefore, we avoid using confident language (e.g., the kind you just read in the previous sentence) when we are making claims about behavior. *May* and *might* are our primary hedge words: "Certain functions may decline with age; it may be fruitful to consider gender in the context of family settings." Sometimes we hedge outside of the verb phrase, for example, "One possible interpretation is . . ." Also, don't forget that hypothesis testing is another excuse for a hedge word. For example, results support a hypothesis; they seldom confirm it, and they never prove it.

 # Exercise 5

List some hedge words from your articles.

1. suggests

2. appears to

3. is consistent with

4. _____

5. _____

Transition words and phrases help to connect the discussion of one study to that of another. They also guide the reader through the logic of the sequence of paragraphs. They can make your writing more precise. Look for them at the beginning of sentences, set off by commas.

 # Exercise 6

List transition words and phrases. These are often at the beginning of sentences, but other words can hold that place as well. When you find a word or phrase at the beginning of a paragraph set off by a comma from the rest of the sentence, ask yourself whether it helps to connect that sentence to the previous paragraph. If it does, put it on this list.

1. Notably,

2. In contrast,

3. Similarly,

4. _____

5. _____

6. _____

7. _____

8. _____

A common mistake is using a transition by itself (such as *on the other hand*) that requires the explicit use of a preceding one (*on one hand*). Also, if you are going to enumerate your points, use *first, second, and third*—not *firstly, secondly,* and *thirdly*. And don't use *second* if you have not been explicit about *first*.

Words and Phrases to Avoid

The *Publication Manual* offers many examples of writing errors to avoid. This section merely highlights some common student bloopers. It would be wise for students also to look over the chapter entitled "Writing Clearly and Concisely" in the *Publication Manual* or "Concise and Bias-Free Writing" in the *Concise Rules*.

Errors We Have Already Noted

1. The *current* or *present* study when referring to someone else's work in your literature review.

2. Authors' first names.

3. Titles of articles in your literature review.

4. The word *prove* (substitute the word *support*).

5. The feelings and thoughts of the researchers you cite.

6. What other authors *stated, said,* or *wrote*.

Wordiness and Redundancy

Wordiness and redundancy are not the same. You should avoid using more words than you need (e.g., *based on the fact that = because*), and you should also try not to say the same thing twice (e.g., *could be perhaps because = could be because*). Your main concern, however, is to eliminate all unnecessary words. Do not bother doing this until you have completed the drafts related to organization and clarity. But by the time you are on your third or fourth draft (we realize that we are asking you to commit yourself to quite a few drafts!), look for words that you can cross out without changing any meanings. Here are examples:

1. *The results revealed that* . . . Omit the entire phrase and start your sentence with the word that would come next.

2. *The obtained data showed* . . . Where else would data come from if it had not been obtained? Just say *The data showed*.

3. *Participants for the study were* . . . Of course they were for the study. Just say *Participants were*.

4. *. . . due to the fact that* . . . Just say *because*.

5. *The reason is because* . . . Just say *The reason is*.

6. *A total of eight participants* . . . Just say *Eight participants*.

7. *The results were statistically significant* . . . This is science you are reporting. Of course you are using *significant* in its statistical sense. Omit *statistically*.

8. *. . . has been previously found* . . . The verb is past tense, so it must have occurred previously. Omit *previously*.

9. *In her study, White (1997) found* . . . Of course that's where she found it. Omit *In her study*.

10. *Distinctly different* . . . Choose one.

Overreliance on Passive Voice

APA style is more relaxed about allowing passive voice constructions than some other styles are. But sometimes writers get so tangled up in sentences that they don't realize how easy changing to the active voice can be. Here are some common examples:

1. *Participants were administered a questionnaire (drug, test, interview, and so on)*. Examiners can administer a test. Tests can be administered. But what do participants do? They *take* a test. They *fill in* or *complete* a question-naire. Perhaps you can't resist the passive voice: They *were interviewed*.

2. *The study was designed by Rubin to . . .* Whenever you have the passive voice verb followed by the word *by*, you have all you need—you know who did it. This type of construction is so easy to switch to active that you might as well do so: *Rubin designed a study to . . .*

Informal Language and Slang

The tone of technical writing is not colloquial, that is, conversa-tional or informal. The *Publication Manual* provides the example of *write up* as an informal, perhaps imprecise, way of saying *report*. Slang is the most informal type of language. Examples include *blooper* to mean *error* and *no-no* to mean *something that is forbidden*. Students usually know that slang is a *no-no*, and they avoid that type of *blooper*. Be on the lookout (that is, *search*) for informal language in your scholarly writing. (Notice that our use of these words is acceptable, since we are not writing a research report.)

1. Contractions are absolutely unacceptable. Use apostrophes only to indicate possession. Remember that when pronouns express possessive meanings, they do so without apostrophes (e.g., its, hers).

2. Do not be afraid to use *because. Because* is a lovely, precise word. *Being that* is a poor replacement. *Since* is specifically made unacceptable for this purpose in the *Publication Manual. Since* is used to mean *after that time*.

3. Use *while* (like *since*) in its temporal sense only. Hunt for *while* in your papers. If you can't substitute *simultane-ously*, change it, perhaps to *although* or *whereas*.

4. Do not be afraid to use *and*. Indulge yourself. *And* is often the best substitute for *while*. See how many wordy phrases you can eliminate by replacing them with *and*.

Long Quotations and Frequent Short Quotations

Because we strive for clarity and economy of expression, there is seldom need for a long quotation. Literary criticism, by contrast, would be nowhere without the long quote. The way someone else says something is vital to what literary critics have to say about it. But technical styles are seldom quotable. If you are reporting on someone else's research, just summarize the author's point. Perhaps the author has used a word in a new way; if so, place quotation marks around that word. The *Publication Manual* has a rule about how to cite page numbers when quoting from another's work and special rules about indenting long quotations (see Chapter 11 of this book).

It is easy to sympathize with someone who would like to avoid plagiarism and avoid short quotations at the same time. Sometimes you may feel that there is no efficient way to convey the contents of a certain phrase (e.g., "responses were scored for speed and accuracy") except in the author's words. One way to solve this problem is to take a stretch and get a drink of water when you feel a short quotation coming on. Then when you sit down to write again, write that sentence without looking at the source. If it still comes out very close to the original, you can put the page reference in at the end of the paraphrase.

Avoid long quotations and frequent brief quotations.

The Editorial We

Students are often taught (in other classes) to avoid the use of *I* and that one alternative is to refer to yourself in the third person: the author. In social work papers, however, that is absolutely out of the question. The other option is to refer to yourself as *we*. This is called the "editorial we" (as distinct from the "royal we," which kings and queens use to refer to themselves). It is common in some styles to use the editorial we, but the *Publication Manual* expressly advises against it. You are perfectly within your rights to use *I* in a social work paper (and you are allowed to use *we* to refer to the authors if your paper has more than one author). Sometimes the passive voice is used instead but with less than optimal results: "It was hypothesized that . . ." Usually, the best solution is to remember that it is not about you. Refocus the sentence on something other than yourself: "The hypothesis was . . ."

Do not refer to yourself as "we."

The Use of You

Do not affect a tone that implies an interaction with the reader. In a research report, there is never a reason to address the reader of the work (as we do throughout this textbook). Nor is it permitted to use the word *you* instead of *one* in speaking of a hypothetical person. For example, "When you reach middle age, your vision and hearing have already begun to decline." This should be written in the third person: "When one reaches middle age, one's vision and hearing have already begun to decline."

Do not call the reader "you."

The One-Sentence Paragraph

Every paragraph requires a topic sentence. Putting a topic sentence at the beginning of every paragraph will help you to achieve a crisp, clear, and well-organized style. Putting the topic sentence elsewhere in the paragraph (as you may have been encouraged to do in a previous writing class) detracts from the goal. If you find you have written a one-sentence paragraph, you must evaluate the organizational plan that allowed this to happen. Ask yourself what the topic of the paragraph is. Is the entire paragraph just a topic sentence with no further elaboration of the topic? If so, perhaps you forgot to elaborate. Is your single sentence really a bit of elaboration belonging to a topic that already has its own paragraph? Then move it. Is it by itself because it is actually all you really know about that subject? Perhaps your paper would be improved if you omit things you know so little about.

Start every paragraph with a topic sentence and never write one-sentence paragraphs.

Unbiased Language

You probably know that it is no longer acceptable to use *he* when you are referring to a person who could be either male or female. The *Publication Manual* advises you not to use the unpronounceable combination forms *s/he* or *(s)he*. It is also unacceptable to switch between *he* and *she* as if either form could be used generically. You may use *he or she* and similar constructions, but sentences become unnecessarily cumbersome when you do: "The participant filled out his or her questionnaire using his or her code number." Of the various alternatives, try to find one that eliminates the need for the singular pronoun completely. Using *his or her* every time you find that you need a possessive is not as convenient as using *their*. However, be sure that you have used a plural noun prior to replacing *his or her* with *their*. It is a very common error to begin the sentence with a singular individual and then talk about *their* score. If you begin with one person, you must then refer to *his or her* score. The solution is to use the plural (people, participants, students, etc.) and then discuss *their scores*. You have thereby avoided both sexist language and an inappropriate pronoun. For the example above, the best solution would be "Participants filled out their questionnaires using their code numbers."

Do not write "he" when you mean "he or she." Do your best to avoid the situation altogether.

Using Prefixes

A few prefixes are used quite often in social work papers. They include *non, pre, post,* and *sub.* Please remember that prefixes cannot stand alone with spaces on both sides. They must be attached to words. They may be attached with hyphens or just attached directly onto the root words. The *Publication Manual* will give you guidance if you are not sure in a given case. However, you can be very sure that if they stand alone, you have made a mistake. If you tested nonsmokers and smokers in your study, be sure you write *nonsmokers* and not *non smokers*.

Do not leave prefixes hanging loose from words.

Incorrect Plurals

Many professors will be annoyed if you do not use the following plurals correctly: *data, criteria, phenomena, stimuli,* and *hypotheses.* The singular forms are *datum, criterion, phenomenon, stimulus,* and *hypothesis.* You will probably never need to use *datum,* but try to learn to use a plural verb with *data.*

These words are plural nouns: data, criteria, phenomena, stimuli, and hypotheses.

Mixed-up Latin Abbreviations

You probably find yourself writing *et al., i.e.,* and *e.g.* a lot now. But where do the periods and commas really go? The commas go after *i.e.* and *e.g.* every time you write them. What about the periods? The periods go after abbreviations. Here's what these three abbreviations mean:

1. The abbreviation *et al.* means *et alia,* which means "and other things." If you remember that *et* is not an abbreviation but rather a Latin word meaning "and," you will remember that there is no reason to put a period after it. By contrast, *al.* is an abbreviation, so it requires a period.

2. Next, *i.e.* stands for *id est,* the Latin phrase meaning "that is." Both letters in this Latin abbreviation are legitimate abbreviations, so they both take periods. When you need this phrase, use the Latin abbreviation (i.e.) inside parenthetical elements and the English phrase (that is) in all other instances. Both are followed by commas.

3. Finally, *e.g.* stands for *exempli gratia,* the Latin phrase meaning "for example." As with i.e., these letters are both abbreviations, so both take periods. Also as with i.e., use the Latin abbreviation (e.g.) inside parentheses and the English equivalent (for example) in all other instances. Both are followed by a comma.

4. Don't use italics with these abbreviations in your own writing.

Learn how to punctuate et al., i.e., and e.g.

Use of Acronyms

An acronym is a "word" made up of the first letters of a group of words. There will be times when you will read or want to use an acronym. You will already be familiar with some; for example, AIDS, IQ, and REM are in the dictionary. These do not need explanations in the text. Others appear frequently in the field and are easily understood by likely readers, but they are not in the dictionary. Examples are CBCL (Child Behavior Checklist) and FACES (Family Adaptability and Cohesion Scale). At first occurrence, these do have to be explained. They must be written out with the acronym in parentheses immediately following to indicate that from that point forward, you will use the acronym when referring to that group of words. Then don't forget to use only the acronym afterward.

Looking Back and Looking Ahead

In this chapter, we have called your attention to some unexpected APA style quirks and some professorial pet peeves. In addition to our own experience with students, we have selected topics based on ideas from our colleagues, some anonymous reviewers, our students, and our own leapfrogging through the *Publication Manual*.

You have learned some conventions about referring to other authors: to refer to them by their last names, to be polite about their shortcomings, and to be mindful of the differences between primary and secondary sources. You have learned to be precise in your word choices: verbs that suit your sentence subjects, words that avoid ascribing feelings to other researchers when their reasoning is what we care about, hedge words rather than overconfident ones, transition words, unbiased language. We have urged you to avoid wordiness and redundancy, informal language and overuse of quotations. Do not call yourself "we," and do not call the reader "you." Be conscious of tight organization of paragraphs, always using topic sentences at the start. Spelling has become a little more complicated for you: You have new hyphen rules to learn as well as some special plural forms. And you even managed to learn a little Latin!

Now that you have learned some of the special APA rules, Chapter 4 will help you review more general grammar rules. In our selection, we hit the common mistakes of students, particularly the problem areas that professors complain about while they have coffee together.

For more information:

Topic	Publication Manual	Concise Rules
Referring to the same study twice in one paragraph	6.11	7.12
Secondary sources	6.17	7.18
Tone	3.07	1.07
Fairness	2.05	
Think, feel	3.09	1.09
Transition words	3.05, 3.21	1.05, 1.21
Wordiness redundancy	3.08	1.08
Passive voice	3.18	1.18
Informal language	3.09	1.09
Since/because/while	3.22	1.22
Quotations	4.07, 6.03	2.08, 7.03
He or she	3.12	1.12
We	3.09	1.09
Prefixes/hyphens	4.13	2.14
Incorrect plurals	4.12	2.13
Latin abbreviations	4.26	3.07

4

Grammar and Punctuation Matters

Grammar and punctuation are critical elements to making your paper sound professional and, for that matter, making you sound knowledgeable. You have put a lot of hard work into researching your topic. Do not spoil the impression it will make by failing to correct common grammar and punctuation mistakes, thereby improving the flow. You want to make a good impression with the paper. In the same vein, why would anyone think that a good impression could be made by turning in papers with careless mistakes, messy grammar, and punctuation that offends?

Some people have a flair for prescriptive rules of grammar and punctuation. They seem to be born knowing how to avoid run-on sentences. Others need to spend time learning these things, and some of these people get to college with a few gaps in their understanding. This chapter contains a review of some rules of punctuation and grammar to which most college students have already been exposed. We have selected only a few rules because social work papers seem to call for them quite often, and in our experience, social work professors complain that many papers they grade contain errors based on the failure to apply these rules. We have provided examples of proper usage in journals of interest to social workers. This is not the place to learn everything there is to know about grammar and punctuation, only those that are most common. You can find others by completing the exercises.

Parallel Construction

Whenever elements of a sentence have the same function, their form has to be parallel. This simple rule must not be so simple, because many students just cannot seem to get it right. Let's break it down. What elements of a sentence can have the same function?

Items in a Series

"The participants were women, over 21, and had red hair." The items in this series should all be nouns, all be adjectival phrases, or all be verb phrases, not all three.

> An example: "Participants were red-headed women over age 21." (This sentence no longer contains a series.)

> Another example: "Participants were female, aged 21 or over, and redheaded." (This sentence contains a series of adjectives.)

 # Exercise 1

Find examples of parallelism in series. Underline the parallel words.

This article contains an example in the first sentence: McCullough, M. E., & Willoughby, B. L. (2009). Religion, self-regulation, and self-control: Associations, explanations, and implications. *Psychological Bulletin, 135,* 69–93.

In the same issue of the same journal, this article contains an example in the first paragraph: Courtney, K. E., & Polich, J. (2009). Binge drinking in young adults: Data, definitions, and determinants. *Psychological Bulletin, 135,* 142–156.

1. These included eating plums, preparing simple meals with plums, researching plums, selling plums, buying plums, and growing high-quality plums.

2. Low self-esteem is characterized by depression concerning bad hair, obsession with ring around the collar, and unwillingness to engage in confrontations.

3. _____

_____

4. _____

_____

Verb Forms

Verb forms must be parallel when they are joined in a series or by any kind of connecting word. There is an *error* in this sentence: "Participants were left alone and were being watched through a two-way mirror." *Were left alone* is not parallel to *were being watched.*

Correct it this way: "Participants were left alone and were watched . . ."

Another example: "Dogs are more influential than cats, thereby occupying more leadership positions." *Are* is the third person plural present tense form of the verb; it is not parallel to -*ing.* Correct the sentence this way: "Dogs are more influential than cats, and therefore they occupy more leadership positions." *Occupy* is a third person plural present form.

Another one: "Participants were asked to read, and they evaluated the stories." Both verbs should be passive or both should be active: "Participants were asked to read and evaluate the stories."

 **Exercise 2**

Find examples of parallel verb forms with conjunctions.

1. Participants completed a questionnaire for the first 5 minutes, banged their feet on a wall for the next 5 minutes, and completed a second questionnaire in the final 5 minutes.

2. The clinical social workers were praised and were given cake by the dean.

3. _____

_____

4. _____

_____

Half-Empty Comparisons

More likely than what? Older than whom? This type of question will keep you from writing sentences that can be ambiguous. If you are using the comparative form of an adjective (the -*er* form, such as *older, faster, or better*), be sure that the reader knows which two items are being compared. In conversation, this is usually not a problem. If you say, "It's more likely to rain today," your listener probably knows whether you mean more likely to rain than to snow or more likely to rain today than to rain tomorrow. Sometimes when you are writing, however, it is hard to remember that your reader is not as well informed about your context or your motives as a listener might be in conversation. So when you write that the experimental group performed better on the posttest, for example, your reader does not know whether that means better than on the pretest or better than the control group performed on the posttest. It is perfectly acceptable to write, "The experimental group performed better on the posttest than the control group did" or "The experimental group performed better on the posttest than on the pretest." When working on one of your drafts, read through just looking for comparatives, and make sure they are unambiguous.

Another potential problem with comparisons is the failure to make the second part completely clear. This violation results in a sentence like this: "Participants rated the soda in the paper cups higher than the plastic." Did they like the soda better than the plastic?

 # Exercise 3

Find sentences that contain comparisons.

This article contains examples: Lippa, R. A. (2003). Handedness, sexual orientation, and gender-related personality traits in men and women. *Archives of Sexual Behavior, 32,* 103–114.

1. Participants associated more positive emotions with the photographs of the house than with those of the elephant.

2. _____

   _____

3. _____

   _____

Agreement

Between Subject and Verb

Subject–verb agreement is typically a problem only when several words intervene between the subject and the verb. When that happens, there is a tendency to allow the verb to agree in number with whatever noun is nearby and feels like the main topic of the sentence, even though that noun is not strictly the grammatical subject of the verb. For example, sample response 3 below (Exercise 4), it might be tempting to write, "The unrealistic nature of the participants' responses to the frightening scenarios were surprising." But *nature* is the subject of that sentence and it takes the verb *was*.

 # **Exercise 4**

Find a long sentence that really has only one subject and one verb. Underline the subject and the verb.

Here is an example (sixth paragraph, fourth sentence): Trentham, S., & Larwood, L. (2001). Power and gender influences on responsibility attributions: The case of disagreements in relationships. *The Journal of Social Psychology, 141,* 730–751.

1. The goal of all but a few (and those few were the only naturalistic experiments ever conducted on communication between humans and mole rats) of Smith's studies was unfathomable.

2. The objectives of the study, albeit obscure and perhaps not amenable to unbiased interpretation by all but a few highly educated social work students, as was common similarly in the research of Castaneda, were altruistic.

3. The unrealistic nature of the participants' responses to the frightening scenarios was surprising.

4. _____

_____

Between Noun and Pronoun

Students come to college knowing that pronouns must agree in number with the nouns to which they refer. However, in writing psychology papers, students often fail to achieve perfect agreement between nouns and pronouns. The problem is most frequent with the possessive *their*. One cause is the effort to use the nonsexist phrase *he or she* as the subject of the sentence and then later referring to *their* left hand, for example. Remember also that *or* signifies a singular, not a plural, situation. The same goes for *each* (each person *cannot* use *their* pencil). This type of error is so common that you should give your paper a read-through just to check every *their* against its referent. The solution will usually be to choose a plural form for the sentence subject and then use all the plural pronouns you like afterward.

The problem also arises in the following construction: "When a child becomes aggressive, they often need a nap." The author of this sentence has mixed up *a child* and *they* and has then gone on to compound the damage by allowing all these children only one nap. Are they sharing the same nap? Here are some ways out: "Naps often help when children have become aggressive." "When a child becomes aggressive, put that child to sleep for a nap." "When a child becomes aggressive, he or she needs a nap."

 **Exercise 5**

Find some sentences with pronouns. Underline the pronoun and the noun to which it refers.

You'll find all you need in the final subsection of this article: Jay, T. (2009). Do offensive words harm people? *Psychology, Public Policy, and Law, 15,* 81–101.

1. We isolated participants by placing them in cardboard boxes.

2. Freud emphasized the individual's need for soft drinks as well as his or her confrontation with sexuality.

3. _____

_____

4. _____

_____

Run-On Sentence or Comma Splice

To understand how to avoid run-on sentences, you will have to back up and understand once and for all what an independent clause is. A *clause* is a group of related words containing a subject and a predicate. An *independent clause* makes complete sense and is just like a sentence. A *dependent clause* also contains a subject and a predicate, but it begins with a word that ruins the whole prospect of looking like a sentence. It does not make complete sense because that little introductory word *depends* on another part of the sentence to make sense.

Independent clause: The participants ate the sausages.

Dependent clause: Although the participants ate the sausages

You may not join two independent clauses with a comma. (If you do, you have written a run-on sentence or a comma splice.) For example: "The participants ate the sausages, the experimenter watched." (Run-on sentence.)

To correct the situation, you have three choices: (1) make two sentences by trading the comma for a period; (2) trade the comma for a semicolon—after all, something made you think these two sentences felt like one; or (3) join the two with a *coordinating conjunction*. Be sure to use a comma before the conjunction. Memorize the list of coordinating conjunctions now:

and   but   for   nor   or   so   yet   whereas

Getting back to the original problem, here are some solutions:

The participants ate the sausages; the experimenter watched.

The participants ate the sausages. The experimenter watched.

The participants ate the sausages, and the experimenter watched.

Exercise 6

Find some examples of sentences with two independent clauses joined by a coordinating conjunction.

You can find plenty of examples in the same section of the article that was suggested for Exercise 5.

1. We instructed participants to sit comfortably, yet we provided no chairs.

2. These results show no relationship between gender and hair length, but they support the results of previous studies.

3. _____

_____

4. _____

_____

The other way to get into trouble with a run-on sentence is to join two independent clauses with the wrong kind of conjunctive word: a *conjunctive adverb*. Here is an example: "The participants ate the sausages, however, the experimenters never saw a thing." *However* is one of the words (conjunctive adverb) that cannot legally join two independent clauses. When you find one of these run-ons in your work, make two sentences out of it: "The participants ate the sausages. However, the experimenters never saw a thing."

Here is a list of conjunctive adverbs that are likely to get you into this type of trouble:

afterward	furthermore	likewise	similarly
also	however	moreover	then
besides	indeed	nevertheless	therefore
consequently	later	otherwise	thus

Notice what lovely words they are when they begin sentences. Use them whenever you can. Just do not use them to join two independent clauses.

Punctuation

Colons With Lists

Sometimes a colon introduces a list. Some students use a colon to introduce every list. However, if you have a word or phrase that indicates that a list is on its way, use a comma instead. These are some common examples:

for example   for instance   namely   that is

The exception to this rule is *as follows* or *the following*. These list-introducing phrases *do* take a colon. Another exception is *such as*. That one has *no* punctuation before the list.

Sometimes a list just serves as the object of a verb: "The participants touched turtles, snakes, lizards, and jellyfish." If you are the kind of person who puts a colon after the word *touched* in that sentence, stop it.

If it sounds as if most lists need no colons, it sounds about right. The only really good time to use a colon (other than with *as follows*) is when an entire sentence (or independent clause) introduces the list.

Exercise 7

Find examples of colon usage with lists.

1. There were three conditions: turtle scenario, snake scenario, and lizard scenario.

2. The experimenter gave these instructions: Complete the questionnaire and draw a birthday cake on the back of each page.

3. _____

_____

4. _____

_____

Comma Before *and* (and Sometimes *or*)

Some students use a *mistaken* rule that looks like this: Use a comma before every *and* and, while you're at it, every *or*. This is probably the result of overlearning this rule: Use a comma before the *and* that coordinates two independent clauses (actually, before any of the co-ordinating conjunctions). Or this one: Use a comma before the *and* (and *or*) that signals the last item in a series.

But no comma is allowed before the *and* in the compound subject or compound predicate (unless there is a series longer than two—if so, use the series rule for commas). Here is an example of this *error*: "The participants read every fourth word, and ate every third olive." No comma is allowed in that sentence—take it out: "The participants read every fourth word and ate every third olive." That *and* simply joins the two parts of a compound predicate. Without the distracting details, it just says that they read and ate. You would use a comma if that was all there was: "They read and ate."

The same goes for a compound subject: "The fourth-grade boys with shoes, and the third-grade girls with hats traded insults." That comma is illegal—take it out. It merely joins the two parts of a compound subject: "The boys and girls traded insults." When you think you need a comma before a coordinating conjunction, find the bare bones of the sentence—the single-word subject, verb, and object—and see how the comma feels. If it still feels good, do it.

 **Exercise 8**

Find sentences with very wordy compound subjects, predicates, and objects. Notice that they do not have commas—unless the compound is of three or more items, of course.

You'll find a great example in the last paragraph of the Introduction section: Frey, L., Cushing, G., Freundlich, M., & Brenner, E. (2008). Achieving permanency for youth in foster care: Assessing and strengthening emotional security. *Child & Family Social Work, 13,* 218–226.

1. This startling claim was supported by a statistical analysis that failed to find a significant direct relation between age and ability to dance the tango but did find significant relationships between age and a positive view of tango dancers and between a positive view of tango dancers and ability to tango.

2. This is assessed by a decrease in heart rate and/or an increase in vigilance in response to pushes and shoves as a consequence of prior exposure to pushes and shoves.

3. _____

_____

_____

Comma When You Need a Breath

It is easy to see why someone might be tempted to use a comma when sentence parts get very long: You need a breath. However, needing a breath is an absolutely illegal use of the comma. If that is really the only reason you can think of, do not use it. Sometimes this mistake results in the placement of a comma between the subject and the predicate—something that no one would do on purpose.

 **Exercise 9**

Read the sentences from Exercise 8 aloud. Even though they have no commas, feel free to take a breath while saying them.

Important Differences Between People and Things

The relative pronoun *who* is for people. You may never use anything else. This sentence contains a common mistake: "The participants that were in the first group rode horses." If participants are people, use *who* instead of *that*.

 **Exercise 10**

Find sentences with people referred to by the relative pronoun *who*.
You can go back to that same section of the same article suggested for Exercise 5 to find two examples.

1. Individuals who went to bed early were likely to wake up wealthier and wiser than those who went to bed late.

2. Participants who did not return for the second session were asked to clean the chalkboards.

3. _____

_____

4. _____

_____

Looking Back and Looking Ahead

This chapter has tidied up some grammar messes. You now know how to avoid some pitfalls that are fairly common. Your constructions will now be parallel, and your comparisons will always be precise. The parts of your sentences will agree with each other, and you will know what it means if a professor complains that they do not. Commas will not appear out of nowhere because they look nice. And because you have learned about one of our pet peeves, your people will be referred to by the words *who* and *whom* rather than *that*.

In Chapter 5, the parts of the research report begin to come into focus with an in-depth look at the introduction. You will see that a good bit of what you have to learn is quite standardized, and once learned, the format can be used for many of your papers.

For more information:

Topic	Publication Manual	Concise Rules
Subject–verb agreement	3.19	1.19
Pronoun agreement	3.20	1.20
Comparisons	3.09	1.09
Parallel construction	3.23	1.23
Comma	4.03	2.03
Colon	4.05	2.05

5

Writing an Introduction

The *APA Publication Manual* directs that the Introduction of a research proposal, research report, or manuscript should contain these components:

1. purpose of the study or explanation of importance of the problem or research, or debates about the issues

2. scholarly review of relevant literature, theory used to explain the problem or issue

3. statement of hypotheses and their rationales; research design to be used

4. theoretical and practical implications

You will find that authors are often very explicit about these items. An article may even begin with the words "The purpose of the study was . . ." The final paragraphs of the Introduction may contain sentences that begin with "The specific hypotheses were . . ." And in between, you will find the literature review and theoretical implications of the current study.

The components of the introduction for a theoretical or review paper vary from those of a research-focused paper. If your instructor is asking for a review of the literature in a specific area, then you must get to the point quickly. The first sentence of the Introduction should be specific and not so broad that it is difficult to identify the area to be reviewed in the paper. A specific example of an appropriate introduction, with a strong introductory sentence, is provided in the following example:

The need for effective culturally responsive treatments has become more urgent as the number of ethnic minority clients continues

49

to increase. Previous research with a clinically referred sample of substance-abusing African American inner-city teenagers found that treatment engagement increased when cultural content was incorporated in the therapeutic process (Jackson-Gilfort, Liddle, Tejeda, & Dakof, 2001). This article amplifies these findings by offering clinical guidelines for how to develop and implement culturally specific interventions that contribute to the therapeutic engagement of African American adolescent males. (Liddle, Jackson-Gilfort, & Marvel, 2006, p. 215)

Now you are ready to write the introduction and address the following elements:

1. topic, problem, question, or issue to be reviewed

2. significance or relevance of the topic, including the practical significance, theoretical significance, and social policy significance

3. statement of the objectives of the review

4. scope of the literature to be reviewed, including the inclusion or exclusion criteria of the literature for examination

5. definition of key concepts or theoretical frameworks to be reviewed

6. conclusion: a succinct statement of the topic/question being addressed

By the way, you are not allowed to use the word *Introduction* as a heading for this section. Begin your introduction on a new page. The *Publication Manual* instructs that you not label this section in your own paper. Its location indicates which section it is. In the publications themselves, however, sometimes the word *Introduction* does appear as a heading. Remember that the *Publication Manual* is directing authors of manuscripts, not printers of journals.

The Introduction section does not include the heading Introduction.

What Was Done and Why

The *Publication Manual* advises that the first paragraph or two of your paper should provide "a firm sense of what was done and why" (p. 27). In a review article, you should indicate what the issue or problem is and why it is important to study or have more information about it. Statistics are often used to establish the importance of the problem area, and this may be done by providing statistics on the prevalence of the problem or how it has influenced practice, a law, or policy. Do not confuse the importance of a problem with your personal interest in it. Similarly, it is possible for you to have little interest in a problem but for research to have established its importance.

 **Exercise 1**

Select several articles from a variety of journals or use articles that have been assigned by your professor. Examine only the first two paragraphs of your research articles, and copy the single sentence in each that states the purpose of the study. If you do not find such a sentence, try the last two paragraphs of the introduction.

1. Accordingly, the primary purpose of our study is to reexamine the family preservation findings of Fraser and Walton (1994), taking into consideration the quality and level of social support.

2. This research was conducted to determine variables that characterize perpetrators who show escalation in abusive behavior during times of stress.

3. Women are more likely to be diagnosed with depression than men. In the present study, we attempted to find a possible ecological explanation for this finding.

4. _____

   _____

5. _____

   _____

6. _____

   _____

 **Exercise 2**

Still looking at only the first or last few paragraphs of the articles you have selected, find and copy sentences that indicate why this is an important research issue.

1. Knowledge of these factors may help identify individuals at risk for . . .

2. The problem under study here has implications for many social work theories as vitally important to the assessment of . . .

3. As knowledge of the consequences of child neglect has increased, investigators have become interested in . . .

4. _____

_____

5. _____

_____

6. _____

_____

Now consider how authors introduce their work. The first sentence of an article is always written with some strategy in mind. The author might want to demonstrate at the start the purpose or importance of the issue, or there might be other attention-grabbing ways to begin. However, beware of the temptation to overstate. There is no need to characterize the special problem you are studying as a national crisis. Your audience is most often made up of professional social workers. They do not expect the tone of their professional reading to be "ripped from the headlines."

 **Exercise 3**

Copy the first sentence from several articles. Indicate what type of information it contains. It is possible that some of the sentences you found for Exercises 1 and 2 held this place of honor in an article.

For this exercise, however, do not recycle sentences from the previous exercises.

1. A shortage of foster homes over the past 20 years for the now 500,000 children in protective custody has jeopardized the quality of services provided to the nation's most vulnerable population. (This is stating a long-studied and serious problem, which is also why this study is important.)

2. Violence, juvenile delinquency, and criminal behavior, especially in urban-centered schools, are characteristic of some communities. (This is a statement of a well-known phenomenon.)

3. Violence is a learned behavior and thus amenable to prevention and change. (This is a definition.)

4. Persons over the age of 110 often flood counseling centers with their marital problems. (Alarming but little-known statistics.)

5. _____

_____

6. _____

_____

7. _____

_____

 # Exercise 4

Now look at the final few paragraphs of the introduction. Find the specific hypotheses. Copy the sentences or phrases that tell you the hypotheses that are being stated. Look for words such as *predict* or *expect* if you do not see what you are looking for right away.

1. Specific predictions were as follows . . .

2. It was anticipated that the ability to express empathy would affect the way in which social work practicum students assessed clients during the initial interview.

3. The use of a genogram and ecomap was expected to enhance parents' understanding of family strengths and weaknesses.

4. _____

_____

5. _____

_____

6. _____

_____

Hypotheses need rationales—they are not supposed to be based on intuition or hunches. It is possible that early in the research process, a researcher did have a hunch. That hunch might even have led the researcher to begin the project, perhaps by beginning a literature search to find support for that hunch. By the time the literature has been reviewed, though, the author is supposed to be able to support the hypotheses with something more convincing than his or her original hunch. Researchers normally use previous results or theories to predict an outcome they expect a study to demonstrate. When writing your hypothesis, you are expected to explain why one group will score higher than another, for example, or why one type of intervention will be more effective than another in addressing a particular problem. This process is implicit in the entire literature review contained in the introduction. But it is good practice to make these reasons explicit at the point at which the hypotheses are discussed.

Exercise 5

Find examples of rationales for hypotheses. Some articles will not provide these in an explicit way just before or just after the hypotheses have been stated. Do not use those articles for this exercise. Find examples of explicit rationales only.

1. If there were differences between flirting and sexual harassment in the workplace, differences between their effects on behavior would be expected.

2. From prior research with adult sexual-assault survivors, trauma-related symptoms were expected to be evident in survivors of child sexual abuse.

3. Because our prior analysis pointed to the importance of avoiding alcohol when driving . . .

This article has 3 examples (or use other articles of your choice): Salomon, K., Clift, A., Karlsdóttir, M., & Rottenberg, J. (2009). Major depressive disorder is associated with attenuated cardiovascular reactivity and impaired recovery among those free of cardiovascular disease. *Health Psychology, 28,* 157–165.

4. _____

_____

5. _____

_____

6. _____

_____

Note that hypotheses often state a direction. That is, they make predictions that one group will perform better than another rather than just perform differently. In Example 3 of Exercise 5, the expectation might be specifically that alcohol-impaired drivers would not drive as well as the unimpaired group—not simply that one group (unspecified) would not drive as well as the other. When hypotheses do not contain a predicted direction of effect, they are sometimes called *research questions*. For example, a researcher might wish to compare two types of support group without a firm belief that one is better than the other. Sometimes these studies are called *descriptive*. In such a case, researchers want to learn how groups differ before they attempt to explain the reason or mechanism for the difference.

At times, neither research questions nor hypotheses are clearly stated in the study. This can happen when the research is at an exploratory level. In these instances, look for words such as *intent* or *purpose*.

Exercise 6

Find examples of the stated purpose or intent of a research study.

1. The purpose of the present research was to examine service providers' perception of factors that help or hinder the process of restabilization among mother-headed homeless families.

2. This study compares child welfare supervisors from majority culture state agencies with those of tribal agencies in terms of ethnicity, professionalization, tasks, training needs, and job satisfaction.

3. The purpose of the study was to examine the experiences of victims of spouse abuse with the police and to describe their expectations for police intervention.

This article contains 3 research questions (or use other articles of your choice): Lippke, S., Ziegelmann, J. P., Schwarzer, R., & Velicer, W. F. (2009). Validity of stage assessment in the adoption and maintenance of physical activity and fruit and vegetable consumption. *Health Psychology, 28,* 183–193.

4. _____

   _____

5. _____

   _____

The final few paragraphs should also define variables and indicate how you have operationalized your definitions. This applies to both dependent and independent variables. You may have used an established procedure, or you may need to explain briefly your own method.

Relevance of the Research Question

In trying to provide a firm sense of what was done and why, writers sometimes have difficulty deciding how much methodological detail is appropriate in the introduction. Find statements referring to the method of the study being reported. Look for *the current study* or *the present study*, which authors use to distinguish their own study from others mentioned in the literature review. (Be careful not to use these words in your own literature review except to refer to the study you are either proposing or reporting.) Notice what issues of methodology the authors highlight in the introduction. They may try to distinguish the special nature of a control group, the elimination of a confound they have discovered in previous studies similar to their own, or some innovation they are contributing. These elements will be described in detail in the Method section but may receive mention in the introduction because they clarify the rationale for the current study.

 **Exercise 7**

Copy the phrases or sentences from the Introduction section that signal information about method. Search only in Introduction sections, not Method sections.

1. The study reported here, using grounded theory method, explored . . .

2. We conducted a pilot study using focus groups to examine . . .

3. Participants were required to read vignettes varying in degree of . . .

4. _____

_____

5. _____

_____

6. _____

_____

Looking Back and Looking Ahead

In this chapter, you have studied the major components of the Introduction section: literature review, purpose of the study, theoretical implications, definitions of variables, and hypotheses with rationales. Although much of this is formulaic and fairly simple to model, the literature review is more challenging. It is the largest section and the most variable. This section will be the focus of the next chapter.

For more information:

Topic	Publication Manual	Concise Rules
Introduction in general	2.05	
Verb tense	3.06, 3.18	1.06, 1.18
Levels of headings	3.03	1.03

6

Writing the Literature Review

A frequent assignment for social work students is to write a literature review in a topical area and provide a critique of that literature. The *Publication Manual* describes a literature review as a way of organizing, summarizing, and critiquing a topic to inform the reader about a problem or issue (p. 10). You can discuss what others have said or reported—what is new, important, or useful; however, it is important to provide a balance of various points of view by assessing strengths and limitations of the literature. You may be attempting to answer a specific question, and this is one way to help determine what literature to include or exclude. And look for "news" as you integrate all the studies into a comprehensive picture of the topic. What is new or different from what other authors or researchers have reported? Identify and comment on the major themes found in the literature and offer a critique of the works. Give your perspective. Your instructor will give you specific directions, but whatever these are, you need to communicate that you have read and understood the relevant research sufficiently to integrate, replicate, and expand what is known on a specific topic. You should cite each study in your literature review for a specific purpose. For example, you may want to stress method in one and findings in another. You may want to know whether relapse can be predicted, or whether self-silencing in women is a risk factor for HIV, or how effective different interventions are for different populations. You should not summarize exhaustively every article you read. You should provide a paragraph or two on some studies and perhaps only a sentence or two on others. As you read each study, consider critically what the research is about and why including it in your literature review is important.

The literature review begins with an introduction where you set out the questions or issues you attempt to solve through the review. Start your introduction on a new page. Type the title of your paper centered at the top, and capitalize all words except conjunctions, articles, and short prepositions. Capitalize all words of four letters or more even if they are prepositions (e.g., with, almost). Do not use the word *Introduction* as a heading for this section. Its location indicates what section it is. State why it is important to review the research, and for what purpose. Set out the aim in this introduction, and identify any issue or controversy about the topic that may follow. The introduction to the review is one of the key sections because it allows the reader to make connections with the research questions and issues. You will remember that the introduction serves to develop the context for the problem you are exploring. A well-focused and careful examination of published literature then follows the introduction.

A literature review allows you to examine the research question, topic, problem, or issue in greater detail by considering what other people have written about it, how they studied it, and what their studies have shown. Before you begin the literature search process, think through the essential steps or criteria for identifying the literature. First, clearly define the issue to be studied. Second, specify the type of information needed to assess or answer the research question(s). And third, determine criteria for selecting sources of information to access. To clearly define the problem for the literature review, address the following:

- What is the social or clinical problem to be addressed?

- Who or what population has the problem or issue?

- How large is the problem or issue and what is the impact?

Finally, go to the library and search the relevant databases. A carefully constructed search should be documented so that other students or researchers will obtain the same results and information if they repeat the process. We suggest that you keep notes on the search attempts for your topic so this may be replicated if necessary. For an example of a detailed literature search using the identified approach, see Thomlison and Jacobs (2006). Under the section, *Looking for Literature to Review,* later on in this chapter, we present a key search strategy.

After retrieving your information you will appraise the articles, analyze and synthesize the information. This is where the real work begins, and it is certainly no easy process. Now, you are ready to organize your findings and begin the writing process. Writing a coherent literature review requires you to assess, organize, and synthesize a wide range of retrieved information.

The Introduction section does not include the label "Introduction."

What Has Been Written or Researched?

You may be wondering what type of information or evidence for your topic is available? There are many different types of articles in the published literature. It is generally accepted that you retrieve knowledge or information about a topic or problem from books, print copies of scientific journals, practice-oriented review journals, perhaps conference proceedings, as well as Internet and other sources. These sources vary in terms of the strength of the information or evidence published and can be evaluated in terms of content and degree of rigor you require for the assignment. The best published sources are peer-reviewed journals where the articles have been reviewed by experts or scholars prior to publication to ensure there are no errors or problems in the manuscript. You will find empirical or theoretical articles, systematic reviews, and case studies as some of the more common types of information. Many journals such as *Evidence-Based Mental Health*; *Research on Social Work Practice*; *Clinical Psychology Review*; *Trauma, Violence, & Abuse: A Review Journal*; *The Journal of Consulting and Clinical Psychology*; and *The Journal of Clinical Psychology* publish excellent articles of the types mentioned above. Your instructor can assist you with the criteria for determining which sources are acceptable for your assignment if you are unsure.

With the electronic databases currently available, researchers have access to large bodies of literature. This ease of access will test your ability to remain focused on a specific segment of the literature presented. Be selective and secure a focus. Many articles will be of interest, but you cannot include everything you find in your review of the literature.

If the purpose of your literature review is to demonstrate to the reader that you understand the central issues related to a specific problem area, you will need to review two types of literature: empirical and theoretical.

▪ An empirical literature review summarizes past research and draws conclusions from many separate studies. Often, this type of review presents a state of the knowledge in an area.

▪ Theoretical literature reviews refer to articles that discuss theories, summarize or critique a number of research studies, or provide a general overview of the concepts and constructs related to your topic of interest (Westerfelt & Dietz, 2005). This type of review helps the reader to understand the conceptual framework underlying the issue. The theory informs the reader about how the problem has been defined and provides an understanding of it. It includes assumptions about the problem that have come to be accepted and the historical development of it. It must also include important and related research.

▪ Systematic reviews are increasingly popular in journals as a special quantitative literature review. Systematic reviews are a formal synthesis of experimental research studies designed to explain how particular interventions affect specific outcomes. Many studies about a particular treatment or program are included and a meta-analytic statistical technique is applied to the group of studies to measure the effect, size, and impact of the intervention. The findings of the group of studies are summarized. Meta-analytic reviews can be complex, and you may find the tables in these articles difficult to understand. This is to be expected as these reviews require advanced statistical skills and exceptional analytical skills to conduct. However, the excellent systematic reviews now available can save you a great deal of time when looking for the effectiveness of an intervention with a specific population or problem. Take note of frequently cited references and obtain these as part of your search strategy.

You can see that there are various types of articles. Retrieving the articles, synthesizing, expanding, and organizing the knowledge, and beginning to write can be a daunting but rewarding task.

 **Exercise 1**

Copy phrases that indicate the main topic of a review article.

1. The two most frequently utilized theories for understanding why battered women remain so long in abusive relationships are . . .

2. Twenty-five years of research into juvenile delinquency have provided four constructs that modify aggressive and violent behaviors: . . .

This article is an example of systematic review (or use other articles of your choice): Jones, L., Hughes, M., & Unterstaller, U. (2001). Post-traumatic stress disorder (PTSD) in victims of domestic violence: A review of the research, *Trauma, Violence, & Abuse: A Review Journal. 2,* 99–119.

This article is an example of a theoretical review (or use other articles of your choice): Bolen, R. M. (2000). Validity of attachment theory. *Trauma, Violence, & Abuse: A Review Journal. 1,* 128–153.

3. _____

_____

4. _____

_____

Although it is always best to read and discuss an original source of information, you will find many articles that contain discussions of other authors' work. Recall that we discussed this problem in Chapter 3. If you are unable to obtain or have not read the original article or research, you will need to cite the work as a secondary source.

Place the secondary source, but not the original source, in the reference list. Within the body of the text, name the original work and provide the citation for the secondary source.

Here is an example. If you had not read the study by Hartman and Laird that was cited in Carlson, Wallis, and Weeks' (1997) literature review, your citation in the body of the text would read "Hartman and Laird's study (cited in Carlson, Wallis, & Weeks, 1997)."

Looking for Literature to Review

When you begin to prepare a literature review, either for its own sake or as part of the introduction to a research report, you will first want to consult an electronic database through your university library's online resources. For example: PsycINFO, Social Work Abstracts (Ebsco), ProQuest, PubMed, ERIC, and others. Recall the difference between you and the laypeople that we stressed in Chapter 1. Your new professional persona requires that you use only certain types of sources for your literature review: peer-reviewed (vetted) sources. As mentioned earlier, peer-reviewed means that two or three other scholars in the field have read the work and recommended publication. You cannot generally cite items from the popular press, and many Internet sources are not appropriate. The Internet sometimes does contain suitable sources, but doing a Google or Yahoo search is likely to waste your time. If you do not believe that, stop right now and do a Google search for *healthy aging*. The first page of our search turned up an opportunity to purchase a new balanced fruit drink, become a member of the AARP, learn more about Centrum vitamins, and provide managed care for a parent. Incidentally, we could also find links to scholarly articles about Alzheimer's disease and predictors of high intellectual functioning in a group of centenarians. We could have spent the same time checking PsycINFO and been assured that all articles, book chapters, and books from this database are legitimate sources for a social work paper.

Does this mean that surfing the Internet is of no use to you? Not at all. The first thing you can do is use it to get a better perspective on the range of possibilities for your topic and perhaps narrow it down. You can try looking up some key words in concept clustering search engines such as www.accumo.com, www.clusty.com, or www.bing.com. If you have a general idea that interests you, you can go to the American Psychological Association website (www.APA.org) and search some key words to get ideas. For example, we just searched for *adolescent self-esteem* and found 178 documents including some on aggression, anorexia, gay and lesbian parenting, plastic surgery, HIV, bullying, and cognitive therapy. We would not even have to read them to get an idea that might lead to a suitably narrow literature review related to self-esteem.

It is a good idea to become familiar with Boolean search logic. Efficiently using "and," "or," and "not" in your searches will save you time and gain you more relevant sources on all search engines. Try http://www.internettutorials.net/boolean.asp for more details. The staff in your own college or university library will also be happy to help you learn Boolean search logic. Also be sure to use a "wild card" character. It works like this: Suppose you use the keyword *adolescent*. You will miss sources that have the word *adolescence*. If you type *adolesc**, you will get all words that start with those letters, including *adolescent, adolescents,* and *adolescence.*

Boolean Search Methods:

- AND
  - Narrows a search

- OR
  - Broadens a search

- NOT
  - Narrows a search so use with care

- Parentheses ( )
  - Allows for more than two keywords or to combine AND and OR in the search

- Quotations " "
  - Allow a search for specific terms and phrases

- Truncation *
  - Can be used to expand a search

If you are planning to surf the Internet (and not just PsycINFO), you have to plan to evaluate the sites that seem useful to you. You must be sure that the source is scholarly. It must have an author, a bibliography or reference list, and a date of publication. Look for a publisher that makes sense. You can truncate back the URL to get an idea of the source—go to the address box and delete characters starting from the far right. Stop at each slash, leaving the slash. Press Enter and see what you have. Repeat the process until you get to the domain name. The domain name will end in edu, org, com, net, us, gov, or a country code. If you end up at a magazine or newspaper (e.g., www.nytimes.com), it is not a good source for you, but it may contain a reference to something you can use. It may be a news story about recent research on your topic. Read the item and see whether you can trace the original scholarly publication through PsycINFO.

It is a good general rule that the domains edu, org, and gov are more likely to contain something scholarly than the "dot com" sites. The second rule to follow is that your sources should be peer-reviewed. More and more, some very legitimate scholarly sources are available on the Internet. For example, this site contains free full-text, peer-reviewed journals: http://www.doaj.org/

Many students have been finding what they think they need on wikipedia.org. Wikipedia is a site that allows any user to edit and update or create an entry. *Any user.* That could be the person sitting next to you in class or on the bus. We would prefer that you trust a social work textbook to define a term to give you ideas on how to narrow it down for a paper. Don't run the risk of using wikipedia.com as a reference on a paper or as a source of information that you choose not to reference.

If you want further help on searching the Internet and evaluating Internet website sources we recommend the following;

http://www.library.jhu.edu/researchhelp/general/evaluating/

http://www.internettutorials.net/

http://www.lib.berkeley.edu/TeachingLib/Guides/Internet/ Evaluate.html

Ultimately, you will end up at a professional abstract retrieval database such as PsycINFO. You will do a keyword search and read many abstracts before deciding which articles to look at for information relevant to your topic. Do not just arbitrarily select the first 20 (or whatever number your professor stipulates) for your paper. You want the best 20, the ones that fit together to make a complete picture of your small topic. You will have to read many more abstracts than that to get a feel for what you need. You might get 400 hits and be unable to narrow down your search. Start reading. You will find some articles that are far from your topic. Revise the search with "not" to reduce the number. For example, you might not be interested in therapy, or in depression, or in neuro* articles. Your interest in adolescent self-esteem might have a completely different focus. Knock out all irrelevant items by revising the search at this time to exclude them. To document your search strategy, record the following information:

- What databases were selected?
- Which search engine was used?
- What other sites were appropriate?

■ How many hits did you get?

■ How did you expand or narrow your search?

Example of Documenting a Search

Date	Location	Search Terms/ Search String	Engine/ Database/ Site Used	Results	Ideas for Another Search
Aug 1/09	University Library	PTSD AND Adolescen*	PsycINFO	531 hits	Narrow search by looking for interventions

You are looking for theories about your topic, findings relevant to your topic, methodology used to study your topic, and literature reviews about your topic. You will not be able to locate all of the sources you would like to read in your library or through your library's full-text databases. If you have the time, you might want to use interlibrary loan. But at some point, you will say, "Enough!" And you will read and take notes on articles to which you do have access.

Reviewing the Empirical Literature

Reviewing what is contained in the empirical research is a necessary step for any student who is interested in understanding the main findings, trends, research designs, and data analysis methods; areas of debate or controversy; areas of research that have been neglected; and suggestions for additional research. From this understanding, you are in a better position to provide the rationale for a current study or the arguments and position taken in your review paper. At the end of the review of the literature, it is important to summarize your impressions and findings and to discuss how the review relates to your proposed study or topic. For example, you might find that there are gaps in the research and your proposed study will address them, or you might learn there are contradictions in the findings and therefore no one best way to address the problem.

To provide a review of several research studies, you will need to collect information from each study to compare and contrast. Basic information on these studies would include the purpose, theories used to explain phenomena, sample characteristics, methods for obtaining the samples, definitions of theoretical constructs, operational definitions of variables, data collection procedures, and a summary of main findings. Organizing the findings within a framework assists you in understanding similarities and differences. It also facilitates classification, comparisons, and connections and helps you to achieve an overview.

When you attempt to summarize the method of a published study that contains several conditions or several similar experiments with small variations, concentrate on one experiment or condition and describe it clearly. Then you will be able to mention the variations very briefly, and they will be clear (Bem, 1995). For example, for a vignette study, you might describe one of the vignettes and then explain that the other groups read vignettes that varied the age of the client or the number of years of experience of the social worker. For a comparison of interventions, describe one intervention and the dependent measure. Then you can briefly note that other groups were identical except for interventions, which you then describe.

It is not usually desirable to note that several experiments were reported and then describe each one. Describe the general method only. Then, as with the description of various groups, you can explain how the variations on the method were accomplished. When you report results after using this technique for describing the method, you will find it easy to compare the results for each group or experimental variation at the end of your paragraph.

 **Exercise 2**

Provide the following information from one empirical study.

DOI _____

Author(s) _____

Date of publication _____

Title _____

Source _____

The purpose of the study _____

_____

The theories forming the background of the study

_____

_____

Sample characteristics and method for obtaining sample

_____

_____

_____

_____

The major constructs in the study and how the constructs were
operationalized

_____

_____

_____

_____

The specific measures used in the study

_____

_____

_____

_____

The administration procedures used for data collection

_____

_____

_____

_____

The major findings

_____

_____

_____

_____

Limitations of the study

_____

_____

_____

You can create a template using the topics outlined above, or you can customize an existing template to best suit your review characteristics. Use the same format for each study in your review.

You may prefer to use this research study available online to complete the above template: Jacobs, R. J., & Thomlison, B. (2009). Self-silencing and age as risk factors for sexually acquired HIV in midlife and older women. *Journal of Aging and Health*, *21*, 102–128. doi: 10.1177/0898264308328646 Retrieved from http://jah.sagepub .com/cgi/content/abstract/21/1/102

Here is an important tip: throw away your highlighters and sharpen your pencils. Take notes! They are easier to access than highlighting when you begin to write. If you really want ease of access, take notes directly on your word processor. Either way, if you quote, include quotation marks and page references in your notes so that you will not accidentally plagiarize when you start writing or have to go back to the source for the documentation you need.

Appraising the Literature

As a student, you might not feel qualified to assess the quality of the literature you have read. Students who are relatively new to a field are unlikely to improve on the criticisms obtained in the peer-review process. Therefore, you don't *have* to find things to criticize (such as flaws in the sample section). Once in a while you may read something that you think is flawed, and you may even be right. You may politely point this out if you have an appropriate context for the criticism.

When you decide what constitutes appropriate sources, keep the peer-review process in mind. Scholars in our field seldom use any other type of material for their literature reviews. Journals published by professional organizations have usually been peer-reviewed. When those same organizations produce newsletters and documents designed to educate the public, they are not meant for scholarly citation. However, newsletters often summarize findings that relate to public policy, and the articles may contain clues that can direct you to original sources: the professional journal articles where these findings were first published. The same goes for newspaper and magazine stories. You may read about some interesting new finding relevant to social work in a trashy or sophisticated source that is meant for the general public. The name of the researcher will be in that article. Use your library database to search out the original journal publication. If the finding was presented at a conference, find out what university the author is affiliated with, use your web-searching skill, and e-mail the author, requesting a copy of the paper.

Speaking of web searching, let's take a moment to point out some commonsense strategies for deciding when Internet sources are appropriate for your literature review. Most web pages are created for purposes such as advertising and entertainment (often known as "dot com" sites). You would not hesitate to omit such print sources in your literature search. But what about something that looks a bit more authoritative? A good guideline is to be suspicious if there is no author or date on the site. Assume that if you find something interesting with no designated author, you should check the facts in a professional journal. You might get some ideas for search terms from unauthored sites. If you find an author and a date, surf a bit to learn more about the site. There are some websites that contain peer-reviewed material that has never appeared in print. Websites that fall into this category will make it easy for you to understand that they are peer-reviewed—they are proud of it. These are likely to be "dot org" sites (the likely sponsor is a professional or charitable organization) or "dot edu" sites (sponsored by educational institutions). Sometimes a "dot edu" site is simply the personal website of a professor; if so, you cannot trust research material printed there. Professors who use their own websites to publish their research may have tried and failed to have it published in a reputable journal.

When you use university library databases that provide full-text articles, you can usually limit your search to peer-reviewed articles only. Wilson Omi-File and Proquest, for example, make this very easy. Note that you often have the option to see articles in HTML or printer-friendly format or in page image PDF format. The PDF format reproduces the article exactly as it appears in print, so you can trust page numbers when you quote. You cannot use the HTML version in this way, although it contains all the words in the original print article.

Synthesizing the Literature

Once you have identified the literature that is to appear in your review, you need to decide how to organize the information. Articles may be grouped according to similar purposes, research goals, findings, or similar methodological issues. From these groupings, you can map an outline of the concepts and studies to be presented in your review. Translating the similarities and differences among sources into the language of hypotheses (i.e., statements that provide the basis for further arguments) will assist you in developing the flow of your literature review. Reviewing what the available empirical literature reveals will assist you in understanding the similarities and differences between previous research and current research. This is known as a synthesis of the literature. Reviewing the literature is not simply recounting what has been done in a long list of studies. It requires you to put them together in unique ways that reflect your critical thinking abilities and highlight the patterns that you have noticed across studies. Many critical thinking skills that social workers learn to use with clients are also applicable to writing a literature review. For example, you need to identify similarities and differences; recognize contradictions and inconsistencies; clarify issues, conclusions, and assumptions; evaluate arguments and interpretations; and identify evidence that supports the degree of accuracy of various sources of information.

A common mistake that students make in reviewing the literature is to include only studies or articles that support their perspective. But a good literature review is balanced, and your written presentation of the literature should contain multiple perspectives, including opposing findings and comments regarding the limitations of your own review.

Let's assume that you have gathered the information for your review of the literature. You have noted patterns across various articles and empirical studies. You have noted the limitations. Now it is time to sift out what is new in all of this. Do the findings in these studies support your study question or hypotheses? How do your findings or analyses apply or relate to your topic of study? If you are preparing to conduct a research study, you must decide what you can apply from the studies reviewed to your own research. It is also wise to consider how you might use the strengths of previous research and how to compensate for the limitations you have noted.

What Was Done and Why

If you look a little more closely, you find that the *Publication Manual* advises that the first paragraph or two should provide "a firm sense of what was done and why" (p. 27).

 # Exercise 3

Select several articles from a variety of journals or use articles that have been assigned by your professor. Examining only the first two paragraphs of the research articles, copy the single sentence in each that states the purpose of the study. If you do not find such a sentence, try the last two paragraphs of the introduction.

1. Accordingly, the primary purpose of our study is to reexamine the findings of Lector (1999), taking into consideration the number of hours of food deprivation.

2. This research was conducted to determine variables that characterize beach umbrella dealers who show escalation in rude behavior during the winter months.

3. Elephants are always larger than turtles. In the present study, we attempted to find a possible explanation for this striking finding.

4. _____

_____

5. _____

_____

6. _____

_____

Organizing the Literature Review

After gathering all your notes, it is time to organize them for your review. Stay focused on your purpose and do not let yourself get sidetracked by peripheral issues. Keep in mind the point you are making about each article and study. This will help you write introductory sentences to the paragraphs containing the details. Students sometimes find themselves stringing together ideas or studies without good reason for doing so. Students often believe they are synthesizing literature by providing a series of summaries of studies and the citations. They first summarize the Watts study, then the Clinton study, and so on. The result is a series of annotations strung together, but this does not demonstrate how the studies are related to each other and what, put together, they mean as a whole. Writing the literature review should move with logical transitions from topic to topic, not from citation to citation. When this happens, the student introduces paragraphs with phrases such as "Smith (1995) found that . . ." or "Smith (1995) also did a study of . . ." An author-by-author or study-by-study account is common in student writing. But it shows that the student has not made connections among the studies in the review. Therefore, *also* is not a good term to use in linking studies together unless you want to make the point that the two researchers did something very similar. Perhaps you have decided to build a case for supporting a theory by adding more evidence. If this is true, then say so. Alternatively, you might prefer to emphasize that one study appears similar to another, but an important difference remains and you want to explain it. Knowing *why* you are including a particular study will give you a much better idea of *where* to include it. In this way, your paragraphs will begin with more natural transitions and have appropriately clear topic sentences.

Your written review should reflect your intended audience. Is it a review to inform or educate the uninitiated, or is it a review for a scholarly audience? Keep in mind that your literature review will contain new observations and news about the articles you read, so it is wise to refer frequently to the intended audience.

 **Exercise 4**

Copy phrases that introduce discussion of specific studies under review.

1. In line with these findings . . .

2. Another puzzling aspect of family dynamics is . . .

3. Although Corey's (1995) findings are indications of support for changing court procedures, Cuvez (1996) reached a different conclusion . . .

4. The results of the Self-Esteem Ratings Scale are consistent with . . .

5. _____

_____

6. _____

_____

7. _____

_____

Your literature review is not the place for your opinions, although they are implicit in your selection and organization of sources. If you find the sample in an experiment to be very small, you can call attention to that fact only if someone else has found different results with a similar but larger sample. Or perhaps the author has noted a problem in the Discussion section; if so, you then have tacit permission to cite the author's own misgivings. You may speculate about contradictory findings, but once again, be careful not to take a negative tone about the work of either author. Try not to write about what authors did not do unless you are contrasting it with what you are about to do or what someone else did. For example, Jacobs might not have tested middle-aged female adults, and Cuvez might not have had a no-treatment control group. You may not mention this just to show off that you noticed. It seldom wins you points with your instructor. If your study contains middle-aged participants, then you can use Corey's results (emphasizing the missing middle-aged group) to provide a rationale for your own hypotheses or design.

Do not forget the rules on verb tense in your literature review. You are reporting on work that has been completed. Therefore, use past tense (found) or present perfect tense (have found). Even your own work has already been completed by the time you report the results, so use past tense when you talk about the purpose of your study, the hypotheses, or what the participants had to do.

The exception occurs when your introduction concerns a research proposal, which students are often required to write. In this case, the research is clearly not completed. For research proposals, use present and future tense in writing about your study (e.g., "the purpose is" and "the participants will").

 Use past tense to describe research findings—your own and those covered in your literature review.

Use Headings

The literature review requires the use of headings. In general, students do not use enough headings in their written presentation of the literature review. Methodological articles or research studies follow APA-style headings. The organization of your review could follow that of any research study: introduction (remember that the overall header "Introduction" is not used), methodology (including how you obtained your sample of articles, inclusion and/or exclusion criteria, etc.), results, and discussion. The results and discussion sections may be combined and subheadings used to highlight your findings. When you just cannot think of a good transition sentence for your next paragraph, it might be time to consider breaking your review into sections. If you have a heading for a section, you can avoid that difficult transition sentence; the heading tells the reader where you are going. But do not abuse the help of headings. For example, do not use headings to avoid logical sequencing. Use them to enhance the evidence of your logic.

Here is where an outline will help you. Although most people are taught that it is appropriate to outline a paper before writing it, few people actually do so. We encourage you to try to write an outline first, as it helps most writers to focus and organize their thinking. You may find, however, that it is easier to outline your paper after you begin to write. Write an outline (if you have not used headings) when you finish your first draft. Be sure to print your draft first; outlining an on-screen manuscript can be difficult and time-consuming. Outline the paper as it stands. If this proves difficult, you have not done a good job of organizing your paper. The topic sentences should guide you in your outline. If they are missing, this is the time to provide them. Outline again after your second draft. If you still cannot do it, ask someone else to try it; if that person also finds your draft difficult to outline, ask why. A good literature review should be easy to outline.

If you have not written your paper from an outline, then outline your paper after it is written.

The *Publication Manual* is very explicit about how to organize your manuscript with headings. (Headings are especially useful in the Method section, and we will take them up again in the chapter devoted to that section of your manuscript.) A manuscript may have headings and subheadings. The subheadings may have subheadings of their own, and so on. These are referred to as *levels* of headings. Students' work is likely to have one, two, or three levels of headings. If you have one level that means that none of your sections has a subsection. Your headings should be centered, and important words should begin with uppercase letters, just as in the title of your paper:

Here is An Example of Such A Heading

If you have two levels that means that your sections have subsections. Your big units are headed as above, centered and contain uppercase and lowercase letters. Your subheadings are also in uppercase and lowercase letters, but they are flush with the left margin and italicized. They look like this:

Here is the Main Heading

Here Is the Subheading

Here is the beginning of the paragraph you will write under this subheading.

Finally, if you have three levels, that is, if your subsections have subsections, everything begins the same way. But your lowest level is indented with your paragraph, and only the first letter is uppercase. It ends with a period. All three levels of heads are shown next:

Here Is the Main Heading (Call it A)

Here Is the Subheading for That Section (Call it B)

And here is the heading under that (Call it C). This is the material that you will write under this section. When you have finished, you can start a new section with another heading like C. When that is finished you may wish to do another, or you can go back to the level above it—B. You are even allowed to have another big section we have called A. The *Publication Manual* will take you through steps allowing you to use up to five levels. But do not try this at home!

Looking Back and Looking Ahead

The key to writing a useful literature review is doing a thorough and relevant literature search. Search exhaustively in the professional literature even if your project is relatively small. Try to get the most relevant articles in your possession, whatever the total number of references will ultimately be. After becoming very familiar with them and taking notes on them, you might find that an organization of the material becomes obvious. If not, think about which theoretical frameworks they rely on, what methodological similarities and differences you find, and what implications they present in their Discussion sections. Develop your subtopics from these areas.

The next chapter is about preparing the Method section. This section is fairly standardized, and you will find that it is easy to write. The main thing to keep in mind is that your reader needs to judge your work on the basis of his or her understanding of your method. Be very explicit and very patient. Do not leave anything to the reader's imagination.

For more information:

Topic	Publication Manual	Concise Rules
Introduction in general	2.05	
Verb tense	3.06, 3.18	1.06, 1.18
Levels of headings	3.03	1.03

Example of Research Proposal/Report Outline*

Title Page
Abstract Page
Text of Body of Paper
Introduction (do not use as a heading)
     Research question(s)
     Significance and purpose of study
     Relevance to social work
Literature Review
     Theories, concepts, variables
     Empirical studies
Method (varies but can be divided as below)
     Participants (procedures, characteristics of sample)
     Research design
     Procedure (e.g., intervention)
     Outcome measures (dependent variable, measurement)
[†]Results
     Descriptive presentation of findings
     Discussion
     Interpretation of findings
     Limitations of the study
Discussion
Implications and Recommendations for Social Work
References
[†]Tables
[†]Figures
Appendixes
     Consent form
     Research measure or instrument

---

*Thyer, B. A. (1994). *Successful publishing in scholarly journals.* Thousand Oaks, CA: Sage Publications.
[†]Do not include these items in a research proposal.

Example of Theoretical/Concept Review Paper Outline

Title Page
Abstract Page
Text of Body of Paper
Introduction (do not use as a heading)
 Problem, issue, topic of the review
 Scope, focus, and aim of the literature review
 Relevance to social work
Literature Review and Critique
 Method or approach to the literature search
 History, theories, concepts, models
 Empirical studies
 Systematic reviews
 Case studies or narrative perspectives
Interpretation of the Results of the Review
 Descriptive presentation of findings: relationships, similarities, differences
 Evidence of convergence and divergence of the literature
Discussion and Summary
 Interpretation of findings: what is known or not known
 Limitations of the review and the literature
 Implications and Recommendations for Social Work
References
Tables
Figures
Appendixes

7

Writing the Method Section

The purpose of the Method section is twofold. First, by providing the details of the sample and procedures, you make it possible for other researchers to replicate your study exactly or to make explicit how they are deviating from your procedure. Second, once a reader knows the details of your method, it becomes possible to judge the reliability and validity of your study. When you understand these joint purposes, you are able to make decisions more easily about the level of detail you must achieve.

A note about the sixth edition of the *Publication Manual*: Starting with this edition, authors are invited to use a supplemental website for their articles where more detailed information can be provided. Some of this detail is the sort that previously would have been in an appendix or unavailable except by corresponding with the author. However, appendixes are still available for this purpose. An appendix might contain important materials, description of equipment, or detailed demographic information for participants. Web-based, online supplemental archives are suggested when direct download might be desirable (e.g., lengthy computer code), when the print format is inappropriate (e.g., video clips), when few readers would require the information (e.g., detailed intervention protocols), and when the print format would be expensive or unwieldy (e.g., color figures or oversized tables).

Organization

It is common for the Method section to be divided into subsections. These will generally include at least a *Participants* subsection (the term *subjects* is now reserved for animals) and a *Procedure* subsection.

This usually refers to the administrative aspects of your study or the processes used in administering or implementing the study. Often, the Materials (if special materials are developed or used), the Intervention Description, and the Measures used will be described in separate subsections as parts of the Method section. When archival data (data files that already exist—i.e., you did not need to recruit participants to provide data) are used, you may see a *Sample* subsection instead of *Participants*. Other information in the Method section will include the research design: for example, how conditions were manipulated (or not), how behavior was measured or observed, how participants were assigned to conditions and whether it was a within- or between-subjects design. You may want to include information about the setting of the participants if it is relevant. You are free to decide how subsections can best clarify your work.

 **Exercise 1**

Look at some research articles and copy the subheadings from the Methods section. Note that in editions of the *Publication Manual* prior to the fourth (1994), the word *subject* was used instead of *participant*. The advice in the sixth edition (2010) is to use the term in common use in one's subfield. In social work you may find a section called *Participants* or *Sample*. You will be safe if you use *participants* unless your group did not provide direct consent, as when you observe people engaged in some public activity.

1. Participants

  Measures and Materials

  Procedures

2. Setting and Sample

  Data Collection Procedures

  Measures or Instrumentation

3. _____

  _____

  _____

4. _____

_____

_____

5. _____

_____

_____

 The titles for the subsections of the Method section are flexible. Use them to your advantage.

Now let's consider the contents of some of these subsections.

Participants

In describing participants who provided data for a study, first indicate how many there were. You must also provide some standard information about them and whatever information is relevant to your particular study. The most basic level of information about participants is age, gender, race, and ethnicity. Report age ranges and mean ages. Elsewhere in your manuscript, standard deviations accompany all means, but this is not the convention in reporting age of participants. Indicate the appropriate unit of measure (e.g., years, months). If you have more than one group of participants, you do not have to report ages for each one unless the groups vary notably or intentionally. But you do have to indicate how many people were in each group by race and ethnicity.

Report age ranges and mean age of participants. Indicate the unit of measure as well as race and ethnicity.

Report how many men (or boys) and women (or girls) there were. The *Publication Manual* cautions against the use of the terms *male* and *female* as nouns. You should use *men* and *women* and *girls* and *boys* (high school age and younger) instead. You can use *males* and *females* if the age range includes both children and adults. Otherwise, use *male* and *female* only as adjectives (e.g., female investigator, male clients, male and female adolescents). Use *same sex* and *other sex* rather than *same sex* and *opposite sex*. Use *people* or *humankind* rather than *mankind*. Don't always write *men* and *women*. Sometimes write *women and men*. (Avoid placing the socially dominant group first.)

Use men *and* women *instead of* males *and* females.

 **Exercise 2**

From the Participants or Subjects sections of research articles, copy sentences that indicate number, age, gender, race, and ethnicity information of participants.

1. One hundred women aged 35 to 55 (*M* age = 40.12 years) participated.

2. Participants were 32 social work undergraduates (23 women and 9 men; ethnicity: 78.6% White, 14.3% Black, 5.4% Hispanic, and 1.8% Asian American) at the University of Alabama (*M* age = 23.71 years).

3. The sample consisted of 17 male and 18 female children of divorced parents and their custodial parents. Children ranged in age from 5 to 7 years (*M* age = 6.31), and parents ranged in age from 23 to 45 years (*M* age = 37.11).

4. _____

_____

5. _____

_____

You should specify the race or ethnicity of participants. The *Publication Manual* is specific with regard to which designations are preferred (e.g., *Asian* or *Asian American* rather than *Oriental;*

Native American [or *Aboriginal*]) rather than *American Indian*, but in many cases the specific Indian group or nation would be best). Remember that racial and ethnic group labels are proper nouns and should be capitalized (e.g., *Black* and *White*). Avoid *non-White*. It implies that White is the standard, and it is also imprecise. Always be sensitive to the changing standards for inoffensive labeling. The *Publication Manual* suggests that you ask your participants about their preferred designations if you are unsure. And remember that "hyphenated Americans" have no hyphens in their spelling: Cuban American, African American, Asian American. This rule holds even if the labels are used together as a single modifier, for example, Italian American social workers.

Racial and ethnic group labels are proper nouns. Capitalize them.

Report information that will be needed for readers to generalize from your sample to a population. Often educational level is indicated. Provide characteristics which may act as limitations. For example, they may be students in social work undergraduate classes at a Midwestern university or clients in a Boston social service agency.

Avoiding bias is important in many types of description. For sexual orientation, preferred terms are *lesbian women, gay men,* and *bisexual women* or *bisexual men.* Avoid the term *homosexual* and specify gender. Also, do not reduce people to their diagnoses. It is better to say *people with bipolar disorder* than to call them *bipolars.* Avoid language that suggests helplessness: *people who reported being sexually abused as teenagers* is preferable to *teen-age victims of sexual abuse.* Do not use *elderly* as a noun; substitute *older adults or older persons.*

 **Exercise 3**

Copy sentences or phrases that indicate the demographic characteristics of the sample that seem to be included for information purposes, not because of special intent by the researcher. Think about why the author reported this information (usually to indicate limits of generalizability).

1. One hundred women (75.9% White, 19.1% African American, and 5% unknown ethnicity, 35 years or older) living in rural communities in West Virginia agreed to participate.

2. The participants were 435 tenth-grade students (67% African American and 33% Hispanic) from two urban high schools who completed an anonymous questionnaire and were paid $10.

3. All children were of middle to upper-middle socioeconomic status.

4. _____

_____

5. _____

_____

Often, participants in research studies come from specific populations relevant to the nature of the study. You may have used selection criteria: for example, marital status, diagnosis, or sexual orientation. They share some characteristic of interest. They may be children at certain grade levels, infants born full term, clients with specific problems, people of specific sexual orientation, children of divorced parents, people with specific test score ranges, people above a certain educational level, people of a certain socioeconomic status, and so on.

Sometimes people are given something in return for their participation in studies. Social work students in undergraduate programs may get extra credit or may participate as one way to fulfill course requirements. People may be paid to participate. You must indicate what, if anything, was given to participants in exchange for their help with the study. Otherwise, you may just say that they volunteered to participate.

After you have made relevant information about participants clear to the reader, begin to use these more descriptive terms instead of referring to them as *participants* (e.g., the young and older adults, the children, the students, the physicians). Alternatively, you can use terms that describe the nature of their participation (e.g., respondents, perceivers, raters).

Sometimes participants are randomly assigned to groups; at other times, the grouping factor is based on some characteristic of the participants (e.g., age, sex, occupation, nationality, diagnosis). If the groupings are based on such characteristics, describe the details of this grouping in the Participants section. By the way, do not say, "Participants were divided into men and women." This sentence is a notorious annoyance to professors. If you randomly assigned participants to groups, it is usually more appropriate to indicate that you did so in your Procedure subsection.

Do not write "participants were randomly selected" when "participants volunteered" is more accurate.

 **Exercise 4**

Copy examples of specific descriptions of participants that indicate selection criteria or the characteristics by which they were grouped. As you do this, think about why these characteristics were noted by the researchers.

1. There were 28 participants who demonstrated disruptive behaviors in the classroom and 13 participants who were diagnosed with Attention Deficit Hyperactivity Disorder (ADHD).

2. The sample consisted of 100 nonprofit organizations dedicated to violence prevention in schools that either (a) used only trained professional(s) from their agency ($n = 30$), (b) used one trained staff person plus trained volunteers ($n = 30$), or (c) used trained classroom teachers ($n = 40$) to deliver the program.

3. _____

_____

4. _____

_____

When participants are not randomly assigned to groups but are grouped instead by inherent characteristics, the groups may differ from each other in experimentally undesirable ways. For example, a divorced group may be older than a nondivorced group, or an older adult group may have completed fewer years of school than a middle-aged group. When it is relevant to the research to demonstrate that these other variables have been controlled or that differences have been noted, a researcher will include a statistical analysis of these group differences in the Participants section. Thus, in this section, you may find descriptive statistics and/or statistical comparisons of means of such variables as age, education, general health, or verbal ability. Alternatively, this information may be reported in the first section of the Results section of the study.

Descriptive statistics about the participants and/or the analysis of group equivalence may need to be reported. When two or more groups are being compared, it is important to know that the groups do not differ on a number of variables that may affect the outcome of the study. Because most social work research does not allow for random selection, researchers cannot make the assumption that any two groups of people will have a similar distribution of characteristics. The question of which characteristics to assess can often be found in the literature. For example, if previous research suggested that the level of physical abuse reported by rural women tended to be more severe than that reported by urban women, residence status is an important variable that is of interest in certain studies. If your groups are not equivalent on important variables, then you may need to use specific statistical procedures to control for the effect of this difference.

Statistics may be reported in the Participants section if they describe preexisting differences between groups.

When some participants do not complete the research tasks, it is necessary to indicate how many dropped out and why. For example, some adults fail to come back for a second session; some people may fail to meet certain criteria after testing has begun. When surveys are mailed to participants, some are not returned and others are returned as addressee unknown. Indicate the number of surveys mailed out and what percentage of the surveys was actually completed. When participants do not complete a study, avoid reporting that they *failed* to do so. Say that they *did not* do so.

 **Exercise 5**

Copy sentences that refer to dropouts from studies or survey return rates.

1. Data were eliminated from 129 participants who completed less than 85% of the questions and from 46 who met criteria for excessive inconsistent responses.

2. Of the initial 300 participants, 45 dropped out of the group before the final session and 22 did not complete the three-month follow-up testing. Data from these participants are not included in any of the analyses.

3. _____

_____

4. _____

_____

Power

Indicate in the Participants section how the sample size was determined. Usually, this will involve a power analysis that will indicate that with the given sample size, the analysis for the main hypothesis had sufficient power to find an effect if one was present. A typical way to construct this sentence is as follows:

> For the main analysis, this sample size provided a power of .8 to detect a medium effect.

Ethics

Researchers are expected to treat participants in accordance with the ethical guidelines established by the profession. If you have come this far in your study of social work, then you are familiar with the NASW Ethics Code. When you prepare your research report you must certify that you have adhered to those standards in the treatment of your participants. Currently, the *Publication Manual* encourages authors to indicate their compliance in the Participants section. A sentence to this effect should appear toward the end of the Participants section. Additionally, authors are required to attest to its truth in the cover letters they submit with their manuscripts. This requirement would appear in the instructions to authors printed somewhere in the journals. In the past, this statement might not have appeared in every case in the Participants section. Compliance with these guidelines would be assumed for all studies published in those journals.

Procedure

The *Publication Manual* instructs that the purpose of the Procedure section is to "describe in detail how the study was conducted, including conceptual and operational definitions of the variables used in the study" (p. 29). There are two points of view that you must be aware of in this part of the manuscript: the researcher's and the participant's. Use the researcher's point of view to describe how the study was organized, and use the participant's point of view to describe the task.

Start with the organization of your study. What were the conditions? Did everyone participate in every condition (within-subjects design), or were people grouped in some way (between-subjects design)? Were they grouped by some previously noted characteristic or randomly assigned? (Please remember that people are assigned to conditions; conditions are not assigned to people.)

Provide names for your groups or conditions that help the reader to remember the key distinguishing features. For example, the *alcohol-information group* and the *no-information group* are better designations than *Group A* and *Group B*. Feel free to give a short name or abbreviation (acronyms are useful) to a group after describing it. The alcohol-information group might be the AI group, and the no-information group might be the NI group. Be sure to refer to the group consistently by that term throughout the manuscript. Note that the names of groups and conditions are not capitalized unless they have been given letter or number names (Group A, the alcohol-information group). Abbreviations are usually written in all uppercase letters (the AI group). Keep in mind that abbreviations should help, not confuse, the reader. So do not overdo the use of abbreviations. If the reader is more confused than helped by a complex set of abbreviations, just use the entire words as labels.

Capitalize the name of the condition only if the name is a letter or a number.

Be careful with the terms *group* and *condition*. Although they are related and almost equivalent in the researcher's mind, they are not linguistically equivalent. People are in groups, but they are not in conditions. Groups can perform tasks, but conditions cannot. It is often best to use the word *participants* as the subject of your sentence: for example, "Depending on condition, participants were told that they would hear A or see B."

Use the term condition *carefully. People are assigned to conditions, not the other way around. People cannot be in conditions, and conditions cannot perform tasks.*

 # Exercise 6

Copy sentences that contain information about conditions or groups.

1. Half of the participants were randomly assigned to meet in face-to-face groups (FTF), and the other half watched videotapes (VT).

2. Participants were assigned to one of the four conditions of the 2 (normative vs. at-risk) × 2 (8-week program vs. 6-week program) factorial design.

3. Each participant saw one of the three taped interviews with the family.

4. _____

    _____

5. _____

    _____

Once you have described how the study was organized, explain the task the participants were asked to perform. Start with the general nature of the task, and then give details that apply to all of the groups. Later, explain how the groups differed. Use the participant as the focus rather than the investigator. That is, state that the participants read, rated, completed, listened to, or watched rather than say the investigator gave the participant something to read, rate, complete, listen to, or watch.

Exercise 7

From Procedure sections, copy sentences that describe tasks that participants performed.

1. Each participant attended the 3-hour violence prevention workshop.

2. Participants read the booklet on how to complete an application for low-income housing.

3. Participants labeled the person in each vignette as deserving or not deserving of government assistance.

4. _____

_____

5. _____

_____

6. _____

_____

Finally, explain the method of scoring if it is not obvious. If a summary score was calculated and used for data analysis, explain how that was done.

Materials and Measures

The term *materials* in this sense usually refers to printed or recorded materials. Audio recordings, video recordings, vignettes, curriculum content, manuals, and computer programs would be included in this subsection of your study. When describing materials, allow readers to understand the task participants were asked to perform from the point of view of the participants while also providing enough information for replication. You may be using materials bought or borrowed (with appropriate citations) from other authors, or you may have constructed them yourself.

When you have used published tests or questionnaires, you may list them in the section on Materials, or you may create a Measures subsection. Give the author and year, as you would for any citation. Indicate what the test measures. Try to tie the terms to your Introduction section, in which you have noted how you operationalized your dependent measures. For example,

> Gabor, Thomlison, and Hudson's (1999) Family Assessment Screening Inventory (FASI) was used to measure problems in families.

If you have reliability and validity information that pertains to your population, include those references as well. Indicate the meaning of the score (e.g., scores range from 15 to 45, with higher scores indicating more severe problems). Use past tense to describe what your participants did (e.g., the participants placed a mark on the letter . . .) and present tense to describe enduring characteristics of a test (e.g., the test measures family functioning in specific domains).

Questionnaires and tests that you devise yourself should be explained more fully. In addition to all the information suggested for published tests, it is helpful to provide sample questions in the body of the paper and the complete test or questionnaire in an appendix.

Researchers often construct scales that require participants to choose a numerical response, for example, from 1 to 5. These may be referred to as Likert scales or Likert-type scales. The high and low points (1 and 5 in the current example) are called the *anchors* of the scale. In writing about scales, use a hyphen between the number and the word *point* (e.g., 5-point scale), and the anchors are italicized (e.g., *never* and *always*). Usually, the points between the anchors (e.g., *sometimes*) are not labeled, but if they are, these labels must also be italicized.

Italicize the anchors of a scale.

 **Exercise 8**

Find descriptions of scales. Copy sentences and phrases that indicate the number of points on the scale and the labels or anchors.

1. Test A uses a 5-point Likert scale with responses ranging from 1 (*almost never or never true*) to 5 (*almost always or always true*).

2. Participants indicated their responses on a 3-point rating scale (*1 = never, 2 = sometimes, and 3 = always*).

3. Responses range from 1 (*not at all true of me*) to 5 (*always true of me*).

4. _____

_____

5. _____

_____

6. _____

_____

Sometimes, researchers use materials that are not measures, such as passages to write or read, lists to check, or videotapes to watch. As with measures, these materials may have been developed by others and you used them as originally designed, or modified them, or you may have developed the materials specifically for your study. Be sure to indicate the source accordingly. In describing these materials, follow the rules of explaining the task from the point of view of the participant and giving enough detail for replication (perhaps in an appendix, table, or figure).

 **Exercise 9**

Look for articles that display samples of the study's materials in a table or a figure. Copy the sentence that refers the reader to the material (table, figure, or appendix) and that indicates the type of material displayed.

1. The participants' family relationships were explored with three questions, displayed in Table 1.

2. A modified scale suitable for the Hispanic population was developed from Hudson's existing measure of family problems. Sample items are presented in Figure 2.

3. _____

_____

4. _____

_____

It is tricky to describe materials that vary by intervention condition before you have described the actual procedure. If the design and materials are interrelated (e.g., different word lists for different groups, vignettes whose clients vary by intervention group), remember that you are under no obligation to have a separate Materials section. You can use a *Design and Materials* section if this happens. In this section, you explain how many groups there were, how participants were assigned to the groups, and what was (were) the independent variable(s) that controlled the grouping. Then the reader will be ready for the information that each group received slightly different materials. Remember that a reader can become confused when there are several conditions that differ primarily according to the materials used, especially if you describe the materials before describing the conceptual differences among the conditions. To solve this type of writing problem, some authors decide to include the description of materials within the Procedure section—or even after the Procedure section. It may be better to leave out a special Materials section rather than confusing a reader with descriptions of sets of materials for various intervention groups before you have explained the purpose of the groups.

Finally, if your participants were deceived in any way, indicate that they were debriefed at some point in their participation.

In some studies, you will find a few paragraphs in the Method section that define important variables, both dependent and independent, and indicate how these variables have been implemented. It is best to assume that the reader of the study will not know what you mean by certain constructs unless you explain each one.

 # Exercise 10

Find and copy definitions of variables. Indicate whether the variable is dependent or independent.

1. For the purpose of this study, self-disclosure is defined as . . . (independent variable).

2. Sense of humor was measured by Curly and Moe's (1968) Laugh Scale (dependent variable).

3. Belonging was measured by participants' ratings of the family photographs on a 9-point scale (dependent variable).

4. _____

    _____

5. _____

    _____

6. _____

    _____

Remember Your Audience

When in doubt about what level of detail to use, always assume that your audience is composed of experienced readers. Do not tell them the following:

1. *How to randomize.* Do not explain that you had one hat for men and one for women and that you put each condition label in each hat and pulled one out every time you got ready to test someone. Just say that participants were randomly assigned to conditions or treatment groups. If additional details are relevant (e.g., there were equal numbers of men and women in each group), state them briefly.

2. *How instructions were phrased.* Do not say that participants were told to complete the questions as fast as they could but to try not to make mistakes. State that instructions stressed speed and accuracy.

3. *How answers were managed.* Simply state that answers or responses were recorded verbatim.

4. *How ordinary materials were handled.* Do not explain that participants used pencils to write their answers and that they gave the answer sheets to the researcher when they were finished. Just describe the answer sheets.

Do not tell readers more than they need to know. Assume common sense and familiarity with research methodology.

Looking Back and Looking Ahead

In this chapter, you have learned some general rules about writing a Method section and some very picky guidelines. In general, write so that others can judge the worth of your conclusions. This means that they must know exactly what you did and to whom you did it. A few readers may want to replicate. Do not leave out anything that will mess them up.

You have to provide a good bit of detail about participants; therefore, some of the pickiest rules for this section have to do with avoiding bias and being sensitive in describing people. You want to give men and women equal treatment, conform to race and ethnic labeling practices for the profession, treat sexual orientation without giving offense, and avoid demeaning labels having to do with illness and disability. Do not presume that you already know how these things are done. The *Publication Manual* is full of surprises. Other picky details concern how measures and conditions (groups) are described. Here, watch out for rules about capitalization, use of italics, and hyphenation.

In the next chapter, you may find that APA style gets even more finicky. The Results section is full of mathematical and statistical material that provides many traps for the naïve writer. Use words—use symbols. Use italics—don't. Leave a space—don't leave a space. Use a number—use a word. Use a hyphen—don't. The good news is that there is a rule for every question you might have. Also, there are many standardized sentences that have to be figured out only once and then can be repeated for the rest of your life. The bad news is that there is a rule for every question you might forget to ask.

For more information:

Topic	Publication Manual	Concise Rules
Method section generally	2.06	
Subsections	2.06	
Participants versus subjects	3.11 Guideline 3	1.11 Guideline 3
Demographics	2.06	
Ethical treatment	1.11, 8.04	
Procedure	2.06	
Gender/sex	3.11 Guideline 1 3.12 and supplemental material at www.apastyle .org	1.11 Guideline 1 1.12 and supplemental material at www.apastyle .org
Stereotypes, Reducing Bias in Language	3.11 and supplemental material at www.apastyle .org	1.11 and supplemental material at www.apastyle .org
Sensitivity to labels	3.11 Guideline 2 and supplemental material at www.apastyle.org	1.11 Guideline 2 and supplemental material at www.apastyle.org
Sexual orientation	3.13 and supplemental material at www.apastyle .org	1.13 and supplemental material at www.apastyle .org
Racial/ethnic identity	3.14 and supplemental material at www.apastyle .org	1.14 and supplemental material at www.apastyle .org
Diagnosis	3.11 Guideline 2 and supplemental material at www.apastyle.org	1.11 Guideline 2 and supplemental material at www.apastyle.org
Disability	3.15 and supplemental material at www.apastyle .org	1.15 and supplemental material at www.apastyle .org

Topic	Publication Manual	Concise Rules
Age	3.16 and supplemental material at www.apastyle .org	1.16 and supplemental material at www.apastyle .org
"Failed to participate"	3.11 Guideline 3	1.11 Guideline 3
Anchors of scales/italics	4.07, 4.21	2.08, 3.01
Hyphenation	4.13 and Table 4.1	2.14 and Table 2.1
Appendix and supplemental websites	2.13	6.03, 6.04
Groups and conditions	3.11, 4.19, 4.22	1.11, 2.20, 3.03

8

Writing the Results Section

The Results section should contain the summary of your findings, including the results of statistical analyses. The *Publication Manual* doesn't ask for much: only accurate, unbiased, complete, and insightful reporting of the data analysis (pp. 32–33). This section should be written in a form that is predictable. Report the statistical tests of your hypotheses in the order in which they were originally presented. Do not give in to the temptation to start with the finding you like best or to end with one that supports your favorite hypothesis. Lead the reader through your analyses in the most logical order, not the most exciting one. Do not *discuss* which hypotheses were supported and which were not; those sentences belong in the Discussion section. It is fine to use the same sentence format for every result that involves the same type of statistic rather than to vary your sentence construction for its own sake.

Report results in the order that corresponds to the order of the hypotheses as presented in the introduction.

Statistics

In this section, the *Publication Manual* is very specific about what kind of information to report for each analysis. Currently, researchers are at a crossroads in terms of null hypothesis testing (NHST). NHST is probably at the core of your own statistics classes and foundational in the training of your professors. However, in the sixth edition, the *Publication Manual* notes that "APA stresses that NHST is but a starting point and that additional reporting elements such as effect sizes, confidence intervals, and extensive description are needed to convey the most complete meaning of the results" (p. 33).

In general, you are asked to report per-cell sample sizes, observed cell means and standard deviations (or frequencies). For inferential statistical test such as *t* tests, *F* tests, and chi-square tests, include the numerical value obtained for the statistic, degrees of freedom, and probability level. Report effect size, if possible in original units as well as a standardized unit (such as eta squared, Cohen's *d* or regression coefficient). Reporting confidence levels is also strongly recommended. Use brackets and the abbreviation CI for confidence intervals. Example: The smoking group had a 17% risk of experiencing rude glances, 95% CI [12.3, 21.0]. For *F* tests, also include the mean square of the error term (*MSE*). Indicate the direction of effect; for example, *Group A scored significantly higher than Group B* is better than *the scores of the two groups were significantly different*. You must report actual means and standard deviations (or some other measure of variability) whenever you report that means differed. These may be provided in a table.

Whenever an effect is significant, report the direction of that effect.

Students are usually required to report a bit more information than the researcher reporting in a journal. For example, after a *t*-test result, you must indicate whether it was one-tailed or two-tailed. Also, you will have to include statistical values for all of your results, even the nonsignificant ones. Please note that the word *insignificant* is not a technical term and does not belong in your paper. If you need to say that the result was not significant, use the word *nonsignificant*.

Use nonsignificant rather than insignificant if an analysis does not yield an acceptable level of significance.

The *Publication Manual* advises that you report exact *p* values to two or three decimal places. Report *p* values less than .001 as *p* < .001. In tables, it may be clearer to use only the rounded values of < .05, < .01, and < .001. This is discussed further in the section on tables. The main thing to remember when reporting probability is to use the *less than* symbol and the *equal* symbol appropriately. If the value comes from a statistical package, use the *equals* symbol (e.g., $p = .023$) and report two or three decimal places. But note this exception: If the statistical package computer printout indicates a probability level of .000, you should write $p < .001$. A p value cannot be zero, so .000 from a statistical package (like SPSS) indicates that the probability has been rounded off. The real probability might have been .0000071. If you drop the last zero in the value on your printout and replace it with a 1 and then you claim that $p < .001$, you have made an accurate statement (.0000071 *is* less than .001).

There are only a few ways to phrase statistical reports. Collect some models now. Note also that statistical symbols are italicized such as *N*, *df*, *t*, *F*. Use only very recent journals for this exercise because the older journals might follow rules that are out of date.

 # Exercise 1

Copy sentences that contain *t*-test results. Note that "*t* test" is hyphenated when it is used as a compound adjective (as in *t*-test results) but not otherwise. Remember that statistical symbols are italicized.

1. Overall mean ratings of self-esteem did not differ as a function of age group, $t(49) = .03$, *ns* ($M = 27.12$, $SD = 1.37$) for 60 to 69 years old and ($M = 28.50$, $SD = 2.01$) for 50 to 59 years old.

2. There was a tendency for managers to rate themselves as more approachable than did their staff, $t(50) = 12.31$, $p = .072$.

3. Independent sample one-tailed *t* tests showed that women scored significantly higher than men on knowledge of abuse and violence at both pretest, $t(29) = 22.41$, $p = .021$, and at posttest, $t(29) = 19.33$, $p = .032$, Cohen's $d = 1.84$.

4. _____

    _____

5. _____

    _____

Exercise 2

Copy a sentence that contains chi-square results. Note that Greek letters are not italicized. Degrees of freedom and sample size are included in parentheses. Degrees of freedom are included for most other statistics as well, but sample sizes are not. You are also required to report cell frequencies, but these often appear on a table.

1. There was a significant relationship, $\chi^2(1, N = 31) = 10.4, p < .01$, between the type of maltreatment (physical or sexual) and whether the child demonstrated internalized or externalized behavior problems.

2. _____

_____

_____

Analysis of variance results usually contain the abbreviation ANOVA, for analysis of variance. The rule for abbreviations is the same for the Results section as for the rest of the manuscript. Introduce the abbreviation in parentheses the first time you use the term, and then use only the abbreviation thereafter. If you do not use the term a second time in the manuscript, do not introduce the abbreviation at all. The abstract does not count as part of the manuscript for this rule.

Introduce abbreviations in parentheses and use the abbreviations rather than the full term thereafter.

Usually, the *F* test is reported for the ANOVA. Students have varying degrees of familiarity with ANOVA results. Undergraduates are likely to have experience with one-way analyses and analyses using two independent variables. Therefore, these will be the focus here.

If you compared three or more means in a one-way analysis, report the results using the term *one-way analysis of variance*. Remember that a significant finding indicates that at least one mean was different. Because this finding lacks precision, authors usually do planned or post hoc tests on these means. Planned comparisons are reported as such. Post hoc tests are usually named (e.g., Tukey or Scheffe), and a significance level is targeted prior to the calculation. You are also expected to provide cell means, cell standard deviations, and an estimate of the pooled within-cell variance. These often appear on a table. Effect size is usually reported as η^2 (eta squared) with *F*-test results: $F(1, 115) = 623.16, MSE = 01, p < .01, \eta^2 = .83$. You can only be sure of finding effect sizes in the most recent journals.

 # **Exercise 3**

Copy sentences from Results sections that report one-way ANOVAs. If planned comparisons or post hoc tests were done, include those sentences.

1. We analyzed mood judgments using a one-way ANOVA. Participants in the elated condition rated themselves most elated, followed by participants in the neutral condition and those in the positively grim condition, $F(2,100) = 21.35, MSE = 7.95, p = .004, \eta^2 = .23$. See Table 1 for means and standard deviations.

2. A one-way ANOVA with diagnosis as the independent variable was conducted. Differences were found for age at onset, $F(2, 98) = 7.69, MSE = 6.95, p = .008$. Post hoc Duncan's Multiple-Range tests ($p = .004$) revealed that persons with nongeneralized social phobia were significantly older than those with generalized social phobia, with or without avoidant personality disorder (APD).

3. _____

_____

_____

_____

4. _____

_____

_____

_____

Analyses with two independent variables require the reporting of main effects and interactions. The safest way to report these is either with both main effects preceding the interaction or with the interaction first. Do not report one main effect, then the interaction, then the other main effect. Again, as with *t* tests, if you say that a main effect was significant (e.g., "The main effect of color was significant"), take the opportunity to say right at that time what the direction of the effect was (e.g., "The main effect of color was significant, with the blue-pencil group scoring higher than the green, *F* . . . .").

Interactions generally leave you two choices for phrasing: (a) "The interaction between age and instructional condition was significant, *F* . . ." or (b) "The Age × Instructional Condition interaction was significant, *F* . . . ." Capitalization rules are somewhat unexpected: main effects are lowercase, but interactions are capitalized.

Do not be concerned that you have several sentences in a row with the same structure. Readers will not be put off by this; rather, they will appreciate the clarity.

Capitalize interaction terms but not main effects.

 **Exercise 4**

Find sentences that report 2 × 2 ANOVA results. Copy what you find, including main effects and interactions.

1. We examined mean cooking times for experimental and control ovens using a 2 (gender) × 2 (condition) analysis of variance (ANOVA). Overall, men cooked more slowly than women, $F(1, 62) = 60.51$, $MSE = 27.74$, $p < .0001$, $\eta^2 = .34$. Cooking was on average 1.1 s slower in the control oven, $F(1, 62) = 40.32$, $MSE = 16.21$, $p = .003$, $\eta^2 = .21$. The Gender × Condition interaction was significant, $F(1, 62) = 29.11$, $MSE = 2.20$, $p = .031$, $\eta^2 = .45$.

2. An analysis of variance performed on these data yielded the following results: group, $F(1, 50) = 18.1$, $MSE = 3.21$, $p = .002$; level of income, $F(1, 50) = 21.4$, $MSE = 32.81$, $p = .004$. The Group × Level of Income interaction was not significant.

3. _____

_____

_____

_____

4. _____

_____

_____

_____

5. _____

_____

_____

_____

Correlation results require the correlation coefficient, r, and the p value. Reporting correlation results can be a preposition nightmare. These are acceptable statements of correlation:

X correlated significantly with Y.

X and Y were significantly correlated.

The correlation between X and Y was significant.

The correlation of X and Y was significant.

Correlations among X, Y, and Z were computed.

The correlation of X with Y was significant.

 # Exercise 5

Copy sentences containing correlation results.

1. The correlation between level of education and use of domestic abuse shelter services was not significant, $r = .17$.

2. The correlation between age and use of postshelter services was not significant, $r = .06$, whereas the correlation between levels of physical abuse reported and use of postshelter services was significant, *r* = .51, *p* = .003.

3. _____

_____

4. _____

_____

You must report means and standard deviations, but you do have some choice as to where to do so. They may be presented in a table, in the text, or in parentheses right after the statistic that compared them.

When statistical analyses are used to compare means, provide all relevant means and standard deviations in the text or in a table but not in both.

Even if you have decided to list means and standard deviations in the text as a way to avoid the difficulties of creating tables and figures, you are not off the hook yet. You face the decisions of where to put them and how to refer to them. You can put them after the statistic that indicates that they are significantly different from each other. If there are two means, use the word *respectively* to indicate order: "Mean scores for meat eaters and vegetarians were 6.10 (*SD* = 0.43) and 5.12 (*SD* = 0.23), respectively." Do not forget standard deviations. You can also squeeze this information into the sentence that reports a *t*-test result by using parentheses. You should use abbreviations for mean (*M*) and standard deviation (*SD*) when they are in parentheses: "Meat eaters (*M* = 6.10, *SD* = 0.43) scored significantly higher than vegetarians (*M* = 5.12, *SD* = 0.23), *t* . . ." Always indicate what the mean refers to (e.g., mean ratings, mean scores, mean number correct).

 **Exercise 6**

Copy sentences from Results sections that contain information about means and standard deviations.

1. A post hoc test showed that race car drivers ($M = 100.00$, $SD = 10.13$) and go-cart drivers ($M = 101.30$, $SD = 8.45$) drove at significantly higher speeds than did bus drivers ($M = 48.15$, $SD = 7.02$).

2. Women had, on average, longer fingernails than men (women: $M = 8.35$ cm, $SD = 0.83$, men: $M = 6.42$ cm, $SD = 0.65$).

3. _____

_____

4. _____

_____

5. _____

Note also that authors are encouraged to report power estimates, particularly when they wish to discuss results that do not achieve statistical significance.

Data Displays: Tables and Figures

Tables typically contain expanded data not presented in sentence form elsewhere in the Results section. However, you may see word tables that, for example, show how conditions were organized or what stimuli were used. *Tables always have rows and columns.* A figure can be, for example, a flow chart, a photograph or drawing that illustrates the stimuli used in an experiment, or a graph. *Figures do not have rows and columns.* Here we will focus on only data tables and graphs. Tables are good for presenting data when you want to be precise. Graphs are better for illustrating patterns in your results.

Tables and graphs should be used sparingly because they are inconvenient for readers and expensive to publish. The *Publication Manual* suggests that some of this material might be better presented online in supplemental materials archives, particularly if the material is not essential to one's understanding of the text, but rather would augment it. You may come across this situation in your reading, but as a student it is most likely that your professor will instruct you to present certain findings in tabular or graphic fashion to give you practice.

General rules that apply to both tables and graphs are specified in the *Publication Manual* (p. 126): It is convenient for the reader to see items next to each other if you intend for the items to be compared. Labels should be close to the items to which they refer. The reader should not need a magnifying glass to read the text. Tables and graphs should be understandable without close reading of the text, so abbreviations should be obvious or they should be explained in a note. Make it attractive, but value clear communication over decoration. Although everything else in your paper must be double-spaced, you can use single spacing on tables if that enhances clarity.

Tables and figures should be numbered in the order in which they are mentioned in the text. The first table that you mention is Table 1 and the first graph that you mention is Figure 1. Tables need titles, and graphs need captions. These are really different words for the same thing. They both give an indication of which variables are contained in them but without duplicating all of the words labeling rows and columns. For example, *Mean Happiness Ratings for All Conditions* is better than *Mean Happiness Ratings and Standard Deviations for Fun Condition, Pain Condition, and Control Condition.* Graphs typically have an *x* axis and a *y* axis. A good caption is often just stated as *Y as a Function of X* or *Happiness Ratings as a Function of Condition and Time of Day.*

Certain types of tables and graphs have been used so often that they have developed canonical forms. These function as templates and you should always look for such an existing format to present your data before inventing something of your own. You can find some of them in the *Publication Manual*, in printed journals, and in two helpful books by Nicol and Pexman *Presenting your findings: A practical guide for creating tables* (1999) and *Displaying your findings: A practical guide for creating figures, posters, and presentations* (2003).

 **Exercise 7**

Find one table and one graph displaying data you understand. Copy the table title and the figure caption here.

Table Title: _____

_____

Figure caption: _____

Tables

Locate the table number in the upper left corner of the page and place the title, italicized, below it. Align columns carefully with plenty of space between them. Note that APA-style tables have horizontal lines at the start of the table, separating each row of headers and spanning the last row of data. There are no grid lines separating rows and columns of data. Use the tables feature of your word-processing program.

Most often, results of significance tests (for example, ANOVA results) should be in the text. However, if there are many means and standard deviations to report, then a table is convenient. Obviously, a table with only three numbers probably presents data that could more conveniently be provided in the text. Means tables should include standard deviations (these can be in parentheses following the means with a note to that effect below). Whenever possible, tables should include confidence intervals as well, using brackets (as in the text) or using columns for upper and lower limits. You will not find examples of confidence intervals very often before the year 2010, or even 2011, because it is a new requirement.

Now consider the words identifying the rows and columns. Every column needs a heading. You can use standard abbreviations and symbols here, for example *M* and %. Often, column headings are organized into several layers (two is usually enough). The bottom headings refer directly to the numbers below them. The one above is called a *column spanner*. It can be used to avoid repeating words that belong to more than one heading. So with a 2 × 2 design and several scale scores to report, you might stack one variable under the other. Here is a sample:

Table 1
Means Scores by Age and Instructional Condition

Instruction Group	Youngest		Oldest	
	Verbal	Written	Verbal	Written

The means in this table can easily be compared across age groups or across instructional conditions. Below this you would provide the columns of data, ending with another line spanning across. Under that line go any notes that are necessary to understand the table. If you need a general note, type the word *Note* in italics followed by a period flush left under the final line spanning the table. Then explain what you need to explain, for example, the meaning of unusual abbreviations. Follow it with a period even if it is not a full sentence. A probability note would come next, if appropriate, and it explains how you have indicated p values in the table. Use asterisks for this: $*p < .05$. $**p < .01$. $***p < .001$. Use only the ones you need and be consistent with it across all the tables in your paper.

 # Exercise 8

Find two tables that display data you understand. Copy the titles of the tables and the headers.

1. Title: _____

_____

Column headers: _____

_____

2. Title: _____

_____

Column headers: _____

_____

If you do use a table, you must refer the reader to it and indicate what will be found there. This is a good time to think about verbs and sentence subjects again. If a table is to be the grammatical subject of a sentence, just what can it *do*? Do tables *contain* numbers? Do they *display* them? Perhaps. Alternatively, the contents of the table may be the grammatical subject; then you must figure out what relationship the contents have to the table. Are numbers *on* a table or *in* a table?

 # Exercise 9

Find out now just what acts tables can legally perform. Copy sentences from Results sections that refer readers to tables.

1. Table 3 presents correlations . . .

2. Table 3 indicates frequencies . . .

3. Table 4 summarizes the results of the regression analysis.

4. Mean scores appear in Table 4.

5. _____

6. _____

7. _____

Graphs

Directly below the figure, type the word *Figure* in italics, then the figure number followed by a period. The figure caption follows that. It contains a short descriptive phrase like a title, but that may be followed by other information of the sort that might be found in a table note. Do not capitalize all major words as you would in a title. For example:

> *Figure 1.* Mean relationship satisfaction as a function of degree completed. Relationship satisfaction was rated on a scale from 1 to 10. Error bars represent standard errors of the means. Asterisks indicate significant differences between conditions, $p < .05$.

Line graphs and bar graphs are the most common types of graphs in journals. It is best to produce your graphs with a graphics program that allows a degree of customization. That way, you will be able to follow many very specific APA guidelines, a few of which are presented here. The independent variable is plotted on the x axis, and the dependent variable is plotted on the y axis. The y axis should be shorter than the x axis (the y axis is often about two-thirds the length of the x axis). The axes must be labeled, and the unit of measure must be included in the label. Lines should be smooth and sharp, and the typeface should be simple and easy to read (e.g., Arial or Helvetica). Type size should be consistent throughout the figure, between 8 and 14 points. Do not use color. Do not show gridlines.

For a line graph, differentiate lines by differentiating plot points. Use clear open and solid circles and triangles as plot points. Lines should all be solid black rather than dashed or dotted. For a bar graph, use simple shading techniques to distinguish between sets of bars. White (no shading) and black are preferable to grays and stripes. If you need a third shade, use diagonal stripes.

Do not label the lines themselves in a line graph. Place a legend inside the graph area to explain the meanings of the shapes of the plot points or the shadings of the bars in the legend. Capitalize important words in the legend.

When referring the reader to the graph of your results, you face the problem of subject and verb again. What can a figure legally do? What relationship do the contents of the figure bear to the figure itself?

 # Exercise 10

Copy sentences from Results sections that refer readers to figures.

1. Inspection of Figure 3 indicates . . .

2. As can be seen in Figure 2, . . .

3. Figure 1 illustrates . . .

4. _____

5. _____

6. _____

Refer to all tables and figures at least once in the body of the paper.

The order for back matter in your manuscript is References, Tables, Figures

Useful Rules

1. Letter symbols (e.g., *N, p*) are italicized.

2. Greek letters are not italicized.

3. Letters that are abbreviations (e.g., *M, SD*) should be used only in parentheses. In the narrative, use the word (e.g., mean, standard deviation).

4. Use the symbol for percent (%) whenever it is preceded by a numeral (e.g., 3%)

5. Use spaces between symbols and within equations as if each term were a word (e.g., $p = .05$).

6. Use numerals for 10 and above; use words for nine and below. *Exceptions:*

   a. Never begin a sentence with a numeral. Look up spellings for numbers in the dictionary and pay attention to hyphen use.

   b. Use numerals below 10 in an abstract.

7. Use metric units unless the nonmetric is more familiar (e.g., 3×5 cards). In this case, put the metric equivalent in parentheses.

8. Use a zero before a decimal point when the value of a number is less than 1, unless it can never be more than 1 (e.g., levels of significance, proportions, correlation coefficients).

9. Rounding off: use two decimal places when reporting inferential statistics. Use exact *p* values to two or three decimal places and use $< .001$ when this is the fact. For means, use two decimal places as long as relevant differences can be seen with two decimal places. Otherwise, try to rescale, for example, by converting centimeters to millimeters.

10. Abbreviations for any measurement you are likely to need are listed in the *Publication Manual*. Note that most, but not all, abbreviations for units of measurement are neither capitalized nor followed by a period. Leave a

space between the numeral and the abbreviated unit of measurement.

11. The plural of *analysis* is *analyses*.

12. *Between* is used for two things: Correlations *between* two variables. *Among* is used for three or more: Correlations were computed *among* three variables.

13. Word your sentences so that statistical results are *not* in parentheses. Many statistical results contain parentheses of their own (containing degrees of freedom, for example). Set off these statistical results with commas instead.

14. Do not use mathematical symbols in your sentences as if they were verbs. For example, the following is incorrect: The number of boys = 17. Write out the word *equal(s)* if you really must write a sentence that uses it. The word *was* works well here. Use the mathematical symbols inside parentheses.

15. Common fractions are expressed in words (e.g., one-half of the sample, three-fourths of the divorced couples), and others are expressed as numerals (e.g., 3 1/2 sessions).

Looking Back and Looking Ahead

We warned you that it would get picky. In this chapter, we hope that you learned to take nothing for granted. APA style even has a rule for how much space to leave after an equal sign (one space). Because this chapter focused on how to present your findings, all of which are the result of statistical analyses, it emphasized how these mathematical terms are expressed in prose. It is certainly a pain in the neck to learn all of this for the first time, but it is very convenient in the long run that everything is so standardized. It means that your reading is much easier. You can now go to any Results section and be pretty sure of understanding the findings that cover statistics you have learned. They will always look the same, if not quite identical to how they looked on your statistics class assignments.

In general, you should include the test statistic, the degrees of freedom, and the p value, the direction of effect, the effect size, and the power. Very often, you will also need means and standard deviations, and these are often presented in tables or graphs. As you write this section, be aware of the need to learn or look up rules about using parentheses, italics, uppercase letters, numbers versus number words, abbreviations, and symbols such as the percent symbol.

The next chapter will cover the Discussion section. You can relax about the pitfalls of writing mathematical and statistical symbols, and you can allow yourself to think about why it all matters. Discussion section woes are more likely to be about how to stretch a few thoughts into a draft that seems long enough to satisfy your instructor. However, in the next chapter, you will find many suggestions for how to discuss your results, and you will be surprised at how much you really do have to say.

For more information:

Topic	Publication Manual	Concise Rules
Results section generally	2.07	—
What details to report	2.07, 4.44	4.14
References for statistics	4.42	4.12
Confidence intervals	4.10, 4.44	2.11, 4.14
Probability reporting of *p* value	2.07. 4.35	4.05
t-test hyphen	4.13 General Principle 3	2.14 General Principle 3
Statistical symbols italics	4.21, 4.45	3.01, 4.15
ANOVA: abbreviation	4.22, Table 4.5	3.03, Table 4.1
Capitalization: names of factors, variables, effects	4.20	2.21
Choosing text, table, or graph	4.41	4.11
Table numbers	5.05	5.05
Table titles	5.12	5.12
Table headings	5.13	5.13
Ruler lines and line spacing in tables	5.17	5.17
Table checklist	5.19	5.19
Table notes	5.16	5.16
Standards for figures	5.22, 5.25	5.22, 5.25

(table continues)

Topic	Publication Manual	Concise Rules
Figure captions	5.23	5.23
Figure legends	5.23	5.23
Figure checklist	5.30	5.30
Statistical symbols in text versus parentheses	4.45	4.15
Spacing for mathematical expression	4.46	4.16
Numerals versus number words	4.31 to 4.34	4.01 to 4.14
Metric system	4.39	4.09
Zero before decimal point	4.35	4.05
Rounding off	4.35	4.05
Abbreviations for measurements	4.27	3.08
Parentheses with statistics	4.09 to 4.10	2.10 to 2.11
Fractions	4.32	4.02

9

Writing the Discussion Section

The *Discussion* section contains three types of material. The first can be called *inevitable.* It is inevitable that the results will be evaluated in terms of the research questions and/or hypotheses generated in the introduction. Each statistical analysis was done in an effort to answer one of these questions or test one of these hypotheses. The results of these analyses have been reported in the Results section. In the Discussion section, you must, inevitably, indicate which analyses lead to what answers or which analyses support or do not support which hypotheses. When hypotheses are supported, you will then, inevitably, refer to the theory or theories that generated those hypotheses. When hypotheses are not supported, you will inevitably admit it and look back to the method and/or the theory for enlightenment. It should be clear that the inevitable part could be written by anyone who really understood the introduction and results.

The second type of material found in the Discussion section is *creative,* and the creative part can be written only by you. This type of creativity is the type that characterizes the creative researcher, not the poet. You need to step back mentally from your findings and think about what else *might* be interesting about them. If hypotheses are supported, are there other explanations that a creative thinker might come up with besides the happy thought that your hypotheses are simply perfect? In the case of hypotheses that are not supported, what possible explanations exist? Would it be reasonable to make a minor adjustment in the hypothesis in light of a given result, or are there confounds in the method? Here, we are talking not about technical problems that result from undergraduate foul-ups, but about real methodological issues that might interfere with the results of the most sophisticated laboratory crew. If your results are entirely unexpected (perhaps even in the wrong direction), you can bring in literature that you have not mentioned in the introduction to place these unexpected findings in a new context. Most of the literature to which you refer in the inevitable part of the Discussion section should have been mentioned in the introduction, but there are exceptions in the creative part.

The third part is *confessional.** This refers to the limitations of your study. You must admit that this is not the ultimate answer to the pressing problem you defined in your introduction. You must explain what cautions are necessary in interpreting this finding.

Discuss all findings using the past tense. Your study is over; your results have been analyzed. Refer to what you and your participants did and what you found in the past tense. When discussing the implications of your study use the present tense. For example, results *support* the hypothesis; limitations of the study *are;* findings *contribute* to the literature; results *suggest;* findings *support* the findings of other researchers; performance on these measures *involves.* There is usually a list of potential individuals, groups, or organizations who may benefit from the study and you identify these here in the discussion section.

Use past tense to describe your results and present tense for statements about implications.

 **Exercise 1**

Select several Discussion sections from articles and look at the first sentence or two of each. Copy examples of opening passages that state whether or not the main hypothesis was supported. When several hypotheses have been tested and several statistics have been reported, you may find that the author indicates which specific result or analysis is tied to a specific hypothesis. However, the Discussion section is not a place to restate the results, but rather to explain and interpret them.

1. One explanation that may account for the results is that children who bully are exposed to various forms of victimization in their homes.

---

*We are indebted to Margaret Gatz for suggesting this term to Dr. Szuchman.

2. When both older parents are present, caregiver stress in adult children is sometimes mitigated.

3. Although these studies demonstrate that social work students have lower anxiety scores regarding research and statistics following a 2-week orientation, additional questions await further research.

4. _____

_____

5. _____

_____

6. _____

_____

Exercise 2

List subject-verb phrases found in the past tense in Discussion sections. Copy these sentences in the spaces below.

1. The results of Study 3 showed that the presence of pets increased interaction among residents.

2. The present study examined the influence of culture and traditions on third-generation Aboriginal adults receiving government aid.

3. It is unlikely that our results were due to lack of teacher participation.

4. _____

_____

5. _____

The *Publication Manual* provides less guidance for the format of the Discussion section than for the others. And because it is more creative and freewheeling than the other sections, students sometimes have difficulty knowing when they have written enough. They sometimes resort to noting trivial shortcomings (e.g., not enough participants) and overbroad applications (e.g., that the study should help teachers of students with learning disabilities). However, it is possible to overlay a format of three unofficial sections on most fairly short Discussions. We will call them (a) a discussion of the results; (b) implications for theory, research, and/or practice; and (c) limitations of the study and directions for future research. Remember that these conceptualizations are used here as guidelines and do not necessarily signal subheadings for your use.

Discussion of the Results

The Discussion section should begin with an assessment of the results of your main hypothesis. Remember we noted that you can be creative in this section. Usually, the entire hypothesis is restated in a sentence concerning its support or nonsupport. You should remind yourself at this point that your study was designed to test a hypothesis, not a theory. A theory probably led to the hypothesis, and support of many such hypotheses lends support to the theory, but you must first deal with the hypotheses in your discussion. Recall that some studies are designed not to test hypotheses that imply direction of effect, but to answer questions, describe characteristics, assess relationships, and so on. When this is the case, the word *hypothesis* will be missing from the first sentence of the discussion. Remember, studies do not *prove* or *confirm* hypotheses. The best way to convert the inferential statistic in your results into plain English for your discussion is with the word *support* or the phrase *fail(s) to support*.

Start your discussion by referring to the main hypothesis. Indicate which statistical result appears to support it or fails to support it.

Recall that some studies are designed not to test hypotheses that imply direction of effect but rather to answer questions, describe characteristics, assess relationships, and so on. When this is the case, the word *hypothesis* will be missing from the first sentence of the discussion, but there will be some reference to the purpose of the experiment as it relates to the statistical analyses.

 # Exercise 3

Select several Discussion sections and look at the first sentence or two of each. Copy examples of opening passages that state whether the main hypothesis was supported.

1. As expected, participants provided with an information kit prior to applying for social assistance completed their application and interview process more successfully than those provided with a first-aid kit.

2. The study reported here revealed strong support for the general contention that intermittent reinforcement of temper tantrums increases their frequency and duration.

3. The present findings fail to support the hypothesis that female sole-parents parent more effectively than male sole-parents.

4. _____

_____

5. _____

_____

 # Exercise 4

Look for statements of similarity between this work and that of previous researchers or other works by the same author.

1. Our results support Hudson's (1997) findings that self-esteem and depression are negatively correlated.

2. _____

_____

3. _____

_____

Exercise 5

Look for statements that show differences between this work and that of previous researchers.

1. Given the data from our study, it is clear that the problem of violence recidivism is not solved by completing an anger management course, as proposed by Harris (1993).

2. _____

_____

3. _____

_____

Exercise 6

Look for comments that refer to theories or theoretical contexts referred to in the introduction.

1. Another possible cause for the higher dropout rates among participants in the parenting classes could be the outbreak of viral infections in the winter season.

2. Consistent with a mediation model, this study showed that . . .

3. _____

_____

4. _____

_____

5. _____

You must acknowledge negative results. What can you do with results that fail to support your hypothesis? In light of these results, you might reconsider the theory. What would be the ramifications of adopting a weaker version of the theory or, more extreme, of abandoning the theory? Perhaps your failure to extend a previous finding sheds light on the population to which it can reasonably be extended.

 **Exercise 7**

Look for acknowledgment of alternative explanations for negative findings—explanations other than the "truth" of the hypotheses or theories that appear to be supported.

1. This assessment tool did not reliably distinguish first-year social work students from first-year psychology students on interviewing skills. It is possible that, contrary to our hypothesis, the selection of these majors is not dependent upon the level of interview skills already attained. Alternately, it may be that these majors are more likely to attract people-oriented students than other majors.

2. Another possible cause for the higher death rates among the younger skydivers in this study could be their refusal to use parachutes.

3. _____
_____

4. _____
_____

5. _____
_____

Implications for Theory, Research, and/or Practice

Implications are the logical consequences and the larger significance of the outcome. If hypotheses are supported, implications are inevitable and should flow directly from a well-written introduction.

The logical consequence of a supported hypothesis is a supported theory. This in itself is the larger significance of the outcome. The introduction will have made plain why this is valuable information. Restate some of these reasons. If hypotheses are not supported, you must think creatively and speculate about practical and theoretical implications. Authors have more leeway in this section than in the others. Try to end the discussion with a paragraph that makes it plain why social workers, or those from other specializations, should find your work important.

 **Exercise 8**

Look for comments that refer to theories or theoretical contexts previously mentioned in the introduction.

1. These findings suggest a limit to the use of empowerment theory in explaining the complex array of symptoms exhibited by women who have been abused.

2. _____

_____

3. _____

_____

4. _____

_____

Remember to discuss *all* of your results. If you just did one statistical analysis, you are ready to go on to the third part. If you tested more than one hypothesis or question, you will return to the first part and cycle through the second part again before going on. Begin the next section after you have discussed all of your results individually.

 Be sure to discuss the results of each of the analyses reported in the Results section.

As a social worker, extrapolating from your study to the intervention implications of your results is very important. Social work research is most often practice-oriented. Social workers want to know how to improve the planning and delivery of services to achieve desired and avoid undesired results. For example, social workers want to know whether your results point to a more precise assessment protocol that they could use, how they might reinterpret problems that people present with, or what specialized services need to be developed for a particular population.

Thus, a specific type of implication can point to a practical application. For example, the significance of the work could be that it provides clear guidelines for how administrators and policymakers in hospice settings should communicate policy changes to frontline caregivers. But not all research has immediate practical applications, so if nothing practical comes to mind, do not force the point.

A relatively easy and concrete item for discussion for the new researcher is the practical application of the findings. Do this if it seems reasonable for the type of study under discussion.

 **Exercise 9**

List examples of how practical applications are mentioned in Discussion sections.

You'll find some here: Powers, T. A., Koestner, R., & Gorin, A. A. (2008). Autonomy support from family and friends and weight loss in college women. *Families, Systems, & Health, 26,* 404–416.

1. Researchers and clinicians should be careful about . . .

2. Social work educators and practitioners should be careful about . . .

3. Multiagency teams need to align more closely with case management functions in order to determine that a less restrictive placement for a child has been attempted.

4. _____

_____

5. _____

_____

Limitations and Directions for Future Research

You should include a discussion of limitations or weaknesses of your study, but this should not be a big part of any Discussion section. After all, if the study were truly weak, you would not have undertaken to write about it. You are far more likely to discuss limitations rather than weaknesses. You should imagine yourself trying to outfox potential critics of your study by acknowledging these shortcomings yourself. This concession has the effect of making the reader feel intelligent for having noticed something before you even mentioned it rather than feeling argumentative about your conclusions.

Can the results be generalized to only a portion of the people to whom this hypothesis is supposed to apply? Of course. Indicate exactly what the limits of generalizability are. It is always possible to question the degree to which research results generalize outside the situation, but is there anything about yours that points especially strongly in that direction? Have you used correlational results to indicate the possibility of causality? Now is the time to remind the reader that this type of conclusion must be made with caution. Is it possible that someone else might have operationalized a construct in a different way than you did? Then admit it. However, feel free to defend your decisions in the same paragraph.

The last part of a Discussion section is often devoted to proposing future research. Remember that this kind of suggestion must come directly from the discussion that precedes it. The limitations themselves often suggest how an improved study might be useful in the future. Sometimes new writers, feeling the need to suggest some future research, propose something completely arbitrary. Be careful about this. For example, following a discussion of results related to color coding of baby food jars for new mothers who cannot read, it is not appropriate to suggest that future research be done on color-blind people or people who speak other languages. A sure sign that you are falling into the trap of suggesting irrelevant future research is a sentence that begins "It would be interesting to see if . . ." Suggest future research only if you can suggest what the next *logical* research question would be. And don't forget the verb lessons you have learned: If "future research" is to be the grammatical subject of the sentence, your verb choices are limited.

 # Exercise 10

Look through Discussion sections for indications of the limitations of studies. List the types of limitations that you find.

1. The cross-sectional design does not give direct evidence of change in the variable of interest.

2. The findings are not generalizable to . . .

3. The self-report method provides only an indication of how people actually behave in the situation . . .

4. _____

_____

5. _____

_____

6. _____

_____

 # Exercise 11

List specific words and phrases that are used to present limitations.

1. One limitation of the study is that Hispanic executive directors may have responded in socially desirable ways.

2. One factor affecting the degree to which the study results can be generalized to other settings and populations is the specificity of variables.

3. We did not control for children's differing problem histories and maturation levels.

4. Three factors threaten the internal validity of this one-group pretest-posttest research design: differential participation period, limitations in recall, and instrumentation error.

5. _____

_____

6. _____

_____

7. _____

_____

 Exercise 12

Copy phrases from suggestions for future research that indicate how the suggestions are tied to the rest of the discussion.

1. As suggested in the current study, future research should focus on identifying the specific needs of older women who have been abused.

2. Continued exploration . . . is necessary to determine which of the competing explanations might account for these findings in other school settings.

3. A study is needed that traces the increases in self-esteem in male batterers who have learning disabilities by comparing two groups over time.

4. _____

_____

5. _____

_____

6. _____

_____

Looking Back and Looking Ahead

In this chapter, you have learned that a discussion has three components. The first points to the outcomes of your hypothesis tests. The second elaborates on these outcomes by referencing others whose results were either similar or different, by stressing theories that gained (or did not gain) support from the current results, by offering alternative explanations, and by suggesting important implications for the findings. The third is the acknowledgment of weaknesses (but there is no need to flagellate yourself to any extreme). These components do not need to be kept separate but can often be effectively interwoven.

Now that the research report has been written, it is necessary to provide an abstract. This is a very short summary that is placed at the beginning of the paper. The format is more popular in the social sciences and the sciences than in the humanities. The next chapter will explain how social workers compose their abstracts.

For more information:

Topic	Publication Manual	Concise Rules
Discussion in general	2.08	—
Verb tense	3.06, 3.18	1.06, 1.18

10
Writing the Abstract

An abstract is a summary. It appears on a separate page following the title page. It is the part of the manuscript that the reader pursues first but that the writer approaches last. An abstract tells the reader the purpose of the study as well as the method, results, and conclusions. Abstracts reporting empirical studies are usually between 100 and 250 words long. Abstracts for review or theoretical articles may be briefer. By the time you are ready to write your first abstract, you will already have read and used abstracts for at least some of the purposes for which they are intended. Understanding what readers need from your abstract is the best way to begin learning how to fulfill these needs. Readers you are addressing include the following:

1. *Someone who needs an overview of an article he or she is about to read.* This reader might be a student doing required reading, an expert who is determined to keep up with what is written in a certain narrow field or someone who was so attracted by the title that nothing would stop the process. This type of reader needs an outline that will facilitate cognitive processing of the article. Technical writing does not depend on surprise endings, and technical reading is aided when outcomes are known in advance.

2. *Someone who is browsing through a journal looking for something interesting.* This reader might be someone who subscribes to the journal (probably an expert) or someone passing time in a library (perhaps an expert in a related field or a student). This reader appreciates that all abstracts follow a similar format so that quick comparisons of content can be made. This person wants to know how a certain article will advance his or her professional knowledge. Will it be relevant because of its theoretical context, methodology, or outcomes?

3. *Someone who is searching an abstract-retrieval system (such as Social Work Abstracts Plus, Psychological Abstracts, Sociofile or PsycInfo).* Students use them to look for sources for a paper; professors look for relevant readings to assign; authors use them to determine which journals are most likely to publish articles such as theirs; researchers look for data on a measure they are about to use; graduate school applicants look for articles written by the faculty of a program they are considering. Sometimes the outcome of these searches is a list of articles that the searcher intends to look at or read. Other times, it is a fact-checking mission and begins and ends with abstracts only. Sometimes it is a fishing expedition, and the searcher must decide whether to examine entire articles.

How can all of these types of readers be served by the same brief summary? There are two parts to the answer. First, the contents are narrowly specified in the *Publication Manual*. Therefore, readers will always be able to predict that they will find certain types of facts in every abstract (for example, the number of participants). Second, the style is designed so that it can stand alone and still be very informative.

Location and Length

Place the abstract on its own page right after the title page. The word Abstract should appear centered at the top in the same font as the rest of your paper. The abstract is one paragraph, but it is *not* indented.

Every scholarly journal contains instructions to authors. The *Publication Manual* indicates that a typical length is 150 to 250 words. This is true for APA journals, but be aware that related fields have other conventions, even while using the APA style guidelines in all other matters. Some journals tend to require abstracts well under 100 words, and medical and biomedical journals may specify a length well over 250 words. Use guidance from your instructor if you are assigned to write an abstract.

The length of an abstract is specified by the journal, in its instructions to authors. It is typically 150 to 250 words in social work and psychology journals.

Contents

The abstract of a research report should contain key facts from each section of the report. To accomplish this, try using one sentence each from the Introduction, Results, and Discussion sections and up to two sentences from the Method section. This guideline should keep you within the required word count while including the types of information specified in the *Publication Manual.*

From the introduction, extract the key element from the portion devoted to the purpose of the study and reduce it as much as you can. This information is usually contained in the first sentence of the abstract. The abstract should identify your hypothesis or research question, often in the second sentence, followed by the procedure used to test your hypothesis or research question (e.g., regression analysis). Be sure to identify the main data source, such as census data survey data, or other sources.

 **Exercise 1**

Copy the first sentence from abstracts that begin with a global statement of purpose.

1. Aims were to determine whether risk factors for maltreatment in the first year of life persisted into the second and third year of life.

2. This article constructs an integrated conceptual framework for understanding community violence based on a content analysis of different theories.

3. Attributions of blame for the first and latest episodes of violence were assessed in a sample of 139 couples who were referred to a mandatory domestic violence treatment program in the southern counties.

4. _____

   _____

5. _____

   _____

You must state facts about the participants that are particularly relevant to the study. Include number, age, and gender at least.

 # Exercise 2

Copy statements from abstracts that provide facts about subjects or participants.

1. Fifty-seven men (86%) from a residence for seniors (aged 65–75) had social functioning impairment during the first year of living in the placement.

2. One hundred women and their mothers who were living in multi-generational households that included a child under age 5 were likely to report depressive symptoms to their physicians and were likely to have problems in caring for their children.

3. _____

_____

4. _____

_____

State the major elements of the method, including all procedures of the intervention and the names of measures. A well-known measure may be included in the same sentence as the participant description. Alternatively, if the method is unusual, it is best to write two sentences: one about the measure used and one describing the participants. Try to mention items or features that might be used as keywords in someone's electronic search.

 # Exercise 3

Copy statements from an abstract that provide facts about methods.

1. Ninety-three 8- to 13-year-old children were asked moral reasoning questions based on an animal fable involving a moral dilemma. A key requisite for such studies is a valid and reliable scale for measuring moral reasoning, an example of which is described in this article.

2. The study group was composed of 296 individuals with a history of state psychiatric hospitalization. One group ($n = 188$) was currently receiving case management services; the control group ($n = 108$) was eligible for but not receiving case management services. Survival analysis models were tested to derive a model that contained the maximum number of significant variables for community living until rehospitalization.

3. _____

_____

_____

_____

4. _____

_____

_____

_____

State the major findings. Do this in words, not in statistics, but include significance levels. You will not have space for secondary findings. Indicate only those that refer to the major purpose expressed in the abstract.

Exercise 4

Copy statements of research findings from Abstracts.

1. Child neglect was associated with more negative views of self as a parent and high scores on the parenting potential scale ($p < .05$).

2. Eighty-eight percent of first-time adjudicated youth receiving 6 months of intense one-on-one prosocial adult supervision and living in family treatment settings did not reoffend in the 36 months following their return home.

3. _____

_____

4. _____

_____

Finally, the abstract contains a statement (of the type found in the Discussion) concerning the conclusions, implications, and/or applications of the study. Choose from the following types of statements: what was demonstrated, what the consequences are of what was demonstrated, or in what way the study should be applicable and to whom.

 # **Exercise 5**

Look at the final sentences of some abstracts. Copy statements or sentence frames that seem to summarize the major points of the Discussion sections.

1. In addition to the better-known measure of service assessment and service use, the family service potential inventory used in this study is an important predictor of family strengths assessment.

2. The findings indicate that child neglect may be a risk factor for more negative views of self as a parent, beyond differences between neglect and non-neglect samples in more general assessments of family-of-origin quality.

3. Findings extended prior research by demonstrating that . . .

4. _____

_____

5. _____

_____

6. _____

_____

 Include the major purpose, result, and contribution of your study in the abstract.

Style

The best way to write your own abstract is to follow the guidelines above without concern for length in your first draft. When you have done that, you will probably find that you have gone over the word limit. Before attending to some of the stylistic elements that will help to shorten your abstract, go over it to make sure that it is accurate and self-contained. This editing session might even increase the length of your abstract, but consider why accuracy and completeness are so important. Many people, as described earlier, will never read your entire article. For their sakes, your abstract must be able to stand alone and to report reliably what is in the paper.

An abstract is accurate and self-contained. Some people will never read the rest of the article.

So reread your abstract, making sure that you have not included information that is not in your article and that you have included the major purpose, the result, and the contribution of your study. If you have extended or replicated someone else's work, reference to that work must also be in the abstract (authors' last names and year of publication). That way, someone following up the work of a certain author will find yours in a key word search for that author. However, there is no references list associated with the abstract. The full reference information for studies referred to in your abstract will be found at the end of your paper in the regular references section.

The *Publication Manual* specifies that third person is preferable to first person in an abstract (This study investigated . . . , The authors examined . . .). It also instructs that verbs are preferable to their noun equivalents (*examined* rather than *an examination of*, *analyzed* rather than *an analysis of*). Active voice is better than passive (*Participants rated* rather than *Participants were asked for their opinions about*). Therefore, reread with an eye to how your sentences can be strengthened accordingly.

Use active rather than passive voice in the abstract.

Now reread again, this time making sure that the abstract can stand alone. Do not use unusual abbreviations. Define terms that a social worker with a different specialty might not know. If you have given your treatment groups nicknames or acronyms, do not use them in the abstract (unless you will refer to them twice in the abstract; in that case, present acronyms in parentheses the first time, as you would in the paper itself).

Do not use unusual abbreviations in the abstract.

After you are sure you will not need to add anything else to your abstract and assuming that you are over the word limit, it is time to see what characters, words, or phrases you can delete. First apply the rules that are specific to abstracts: Use numerals instead of words for numbers under 10, unless they begin a sentence; use abbreviations in the text that would normally be allowed only within parentheses (such as *etc.* or *vs.*); use abbreviations or acronyms that are commonly understood by social workers even if you are using the terms only once (e.g., ANOVA and CBCL).

Next look for phrases that are not dense with information and try to omit them. For example, omit "the results revealed that" and "the conclusions are that." Omit phrases that repeat information provided by the title of the paper.

See whether sentences can be combined to save words. For example, perhaps you can include subject and method information in one sentence: "Undergraduate students (25 men and 25 women) rated five types of practicum exercises." You might be able to combine purpose and results by reordering and combining: "The hypothesis that concrete learners prefer nonwriting course assignments was supported in a study that assessed the preferred learning styles of undergraduate social work students."

Do not be discouraged if you are still over the limit. Writing an abstract is a difficult task. Deleting words and phrases that have been written with great effort is an emotional and intellectual strain. Consider trading abstracts with another student if you still cannot find a place to delete words. It is often easier to delete phrases from someone else's work than from your own.

When you finally feel that your abstract fulfills all the criteria discussed so far, you have only one task left: Imagine all the people who might search an abstract-retrieval database and be glad to find your abstract. What key words would these various people be likely to use in their searches? Make sure that all those words are actually in your abstract so that all these potential searchers will find your work.

 Include all the words that someone doing a key word search would be likely to need.

Looking Back and Looking Ahead

Remember the five "Cs": an abstract is correct (self-)contained, concise, and coherent, and it covers all the bases. The specifics follow from those: use numbers, abbreviations, active voice. And make it short. Some journals and conference submissions even require 50-word abstracts.

In the next chapter, trivia (that you thought had been left behind with the Results section) will return to your world. The APA format for references must be followed down to the last comma and ampersand (&). Enjoy!

For more information:

Topic	Publication Manual	Concise Rules
Abstract contents, location, length, format	2.04	—
Numbers as numerals, not words	4.31	4.01
Verbs: Active voice, present tense	2.04	—

11
Listing References

Students often notice that APA style calls for a *References* section rather than a *Bibliography*. The difference is important. In your References section, you list the works you have referred to in your paper. A bibliography is usually more extensive than a references list and may contain material that you read but did not cite. Your references list should be in one-to-one correspondence with the authors you have mentioned in your paper. It should be accurate; readers might wish to consult some of your sources for their own edification. It should not contain anything that you did not actually have in front of your eyes; secondary sources should be listed when appropriate, rather than primary sources that you did not read.

Include in the References section only those sources that you cited in your paper and only those that you actually consulted.

If you read only one chapter of a book, you must list only that chapter. Usually, this occurs in the case of an edited book with chapters by various authors. Sometimes, however, you will consult part of a book written by a single author. In this case, the *Publication Manual* provides specific formats for indicating which chapter and/or pages you consulted.

There are so many types of material that may be consulted that it is not necessary (or rather, not possible) to familiarize yourself with how to cite all of them until you need them. In this chapter, you will learn about the three most common types of references that occur in student papers: journal articles, chapters in edited books, and authored books (the same person[s] wrote the whole book). We also provide hints for interviews and other archival sources. For all other types of references, please consult the *Publication Manual* for details.

Word Processing Tips

- The References section begins on a new page. The heading, References, is at the top of the page and with the first letter capitalized. This heading is not typed in bold face. The rest of the manuscript (with the exception of the Abstract and the items that come after the references) is continuous; that is, no other section begins at the top of a page unless it happens to fall that way.

- Double-space everything on these pages, both within and between references on the list.

- Each entry should begin with a *hanging indent*. That means the first word is at the left margin and all other lines for that reference are indented ½ inch. Do not space-space-space your way through these indents. Format it with your word processor. In Microsoft Word you'll find the command in the Format Paragraph menu. Go to the box labeled *special* and choose *hanging*. Start the same way with Corel Word Perfect and when you get to the Format Paragraph menu, click on *hanging indent*. Many people find that it helps to prepare the References section in block form, with no indent at all. Just press *enter* for each new entry. When you are finished, you can select the whole section and format it as explained above. Remember, if you choose this strategy, double-space throughout. Don't allow automatic spacing between paragraphs. Choose zero point spacing before and after paragraphs.

- Never type authors' first or middle names. Use only their initials and leave a space between initials.

Alphabetizing

Alphabetize according to the last name of the author who is listed first in each source. Remember, use initials, not full given names. Keep the following items in mind:

- Do not rearrange the order of authorship of any given article or chapter. If the article lists the authors as Smith, R. T., & Jones, A. L., do not list them as Jones, A. L., & Smith, R. T.

- Works by the same author are listed by year of publication; works by the exact same group of authors are listed by year of publication, the earliest first. If that rule fails (because they are the same year), alphabetize by title, but don't count *The* or *A*. Then put lowercase letters immediately after the year, and refer to the work in your paper by the year and letter: Smith (2010a).

- If you have the same author listed first with different coauthors for different articles, arrange the entries alphabetically within the listing for that author according to the second author of each entry. List Smith, R. T. & Jones, A. L. before Smith, R. T., & Marks, B. J.

- If an author appears as a single author of one source and the first coauthor of another, list the single-author source first, then the one with the coauthor (following the principle that "nothing" goes before "something"). List Smith, R. T. before Smith, R. T., & Jones, A. L.

Exercise 1

Copy from a list of references two listings by the same author for works published in different years.

_____

_____

_____

_____

Copy two listings in which publications by two or more authors are headed by the same author.

_____

_____

_____

_____

Journal Article Reference

Author(s). (Year). Article title. *Journal Title, volume number,* page numbers. doi:

Here are the rules:

1. Author(s), last name followed by initial(s).

   ◼ Use the ampersand (&) before the last author.

   ◼ Place a comma between author names.

   ◼ Place the comma before the ampersand, even if there are only two authors in the list.

2. Year of publication.

   ◼ Place it in parentheses.

   ◼ Follow with a period.

3. Title of the article.

   ◼ Capitalize only the first word in the title and the first word after a colon (even if these are only little words like *the*), when applicable.

   ◼ Follow this with a period.

4. Title of the journal.

   ◼ Capitalize each important word. This includes all words except conjuctions, articles, and prepositions of three letters or fewer.

   ◼ Italicize the title of the journal.

   ◼ Follow this with a comma.

5. Volume number of the journal.

   ◼ Italicize it.

   ◼ Follow it with another comma.

6. Issue number.

   ◼ Almost never include this. Do so only if each issue of the year starts with page 1. Usually, scholarly journals begin each *year* with page 1, and each *issue* begins with the page that follows the last one in the previous issue.

- If you should have to include this, place it in parentheses after the volume number.

- Do not italicize it.

7. Page numbers.

- Include the full range (e.g., use 125–127 rather than 125–7 or 125–27).

- Do not italicize the page numbers.

- End the entry with a period.

8. Digital object identifier (DOI)

- You may have noticed that retrieving from the Internet is unreliable. Here today, gone tomorrow. The DOI will never do you wrong. If the article is available electronically, the DOI will always be attached to that article, no matter what database you find it in.

- The DOI is an alphanumeric string located on the first page, near the copyright information.

- When you have a DOI, type *doi:* after the final period that comes after the page number. Then type it carefully or cut and paste it. Don't put any punctuation after it.

Journal article examples:

- One author:
  Rogers, M. (2000). My sweater has a zipper. *Children's Television Review, 12,* 120–122. doi:10.1037 /a0013373

- With two authors, use an ampersand and comma between them:
  Rogers, M., & Kermit, F. (2002). Not all sweaters have zippers. *Children's Television Review, 14,* 12–30. doi:10.1037/a0013349

- With three authors:
  Rogers, M., McDonald, R., & Kermit, F. (2002). Not all creatures wear sweaters. *Children's Television Review, 17,* 124–130. doi:10.1037/a0013470

- All of those rules work for one to seven authors. With more than seven authors there is trouble. Name the first six, then three ellipses (. . .), then the last author:

Rogers, M., McDonald, R., Kermit, F., Bird, B., Mouse, M., Szuchman, L., . . . Thomlison, B. (2000). What a pain in the neck. *Journal of Too Many Rules, 7,* 413–414. doi:10.1037/a0013349

 # Exercise 2

Copy one listing for an article from a journal.

_____

_____

Chapter in an Edited Book

Chapter Author(s). (Year). Chapter title. In Book Author(s) (Ed[s].), *Book title* (page numbers of chapter). Place of Publication: Publishing company. (Use DOI if available.)

Here are the rules:

1. Chapter author(s)' last name(s) followed by initials.

   ▪ Same rules as for journal article.

2. Year of publication.

   ▪ Same rules as for journal article.

3. Title of the chapter.

   ▪ Same rules as for journal article.

4. The word *In.*

5. Editor(s)' name(s).

   ▪ Initial(s) then last name—not last name first.

   ▪ Separated by commas and ampersand as for authors, but no comma for only two authors.

6. (Ed.) or (Eds.).

   ▪ Follow with a comma.

7. Title of the book.

   ▪ Italicize it.

   ▪ Capitalize only the first word in the title and the first word after a colon, when applicable.

8. Page numbers of chapter.

   ▪ Use the form pp. xx–xx.

   ▪ In parentheses.

   ▪ Follow with a period.

9. Place of publication.

   ▪ City and state or city and country.

   ▪ Use postal abbreviations for state.

   ▪ Follow with a colon.

10. Publishing company.

    ▪ Can be brief, for example, omit *Co., Inc., Publishers.*

    ▪ If same as author (e.g., American Psychiatric Association), use the word *Author* in place of publisher's name.

    ▪ End with a period

Chapter in an edited book example:

Smith, T. J., & Jones, R. N. (1971). Very interesting stuff: Relationship between grades and dental cavities. In J. Lennon & P. McCartney (Eds.), *A big book of interesting stuff* (pp. 22–125). London, England: British Publishing Co.

 **Exercise 3**

Copy one listing from a References section for a chapter in an edited book.

_____

_____

An Authored Book

Author(s). (year). *Title*. City: Publisher. (Continue to use DOI if available.)

This is a book written entirely by the same author(s) rather than with chapters contributed by various people.

Authored book example:

> Smart, I. M. (1995). *Fun with social work*. Green Hill, IL: Green Publishing Co.

 **Exercise 4**

Write the listing for this book as it would appear in a References section.

_____

_____

Electronic References

In most cases, you will be able to follow the rules above: author, date, title, and so on. Include as much of this as possible and then add the electronic retrieval information. If you have a DOI, that is all the retrieval information you need. Otherwise, you'll need the URL. If you are pretty sure that the source will not change, you don't need the retrieval date. If it is the type of source that does change, like a Wiki, you'll need the retrieval date as well. I hope you will not use those sources.

Here is an example:

> Simpson, B. (1999). Cartooning and casework. Belmont, CA: Council on Social Work Education. Retrieved from http://www.cswedc.org/simpson.html

The best case is the electronic version of a print journal article that you download as a PDF file. All the usual information will be there. You are looking at an exact copy of a journal article. Usually it is also available in print, so you have finished the job. If the journal is not available in print and you used a PDF, and if there is *no* DOI, then you have to find the home page URL of the journal. Don't use the database that you found it on. Search the web to find the homepage of the actual publisher.

For example, say we need to know about early maternal separation and how it relates to symptoms of activity-based anorexia in male and female rats. This 2009 article by Hancock and Grant is in the *Journal of Experimental Psychology: Animal Behavior Processes*. We can obtain it at no cost from the university library's online journal collection. The university subscribes to a database called PsycARTICLES and we can link to the article from there. There is a DOI: 10.1037/a0014736. So we just read the PDF version, reference it the normal way, and include the DOI. If there were no DOI, we would have to notice that it is published by APA, and we would go to APA .org and start surfing till we find the abstract at http://psycnet.apa .org/index.cfm?fa=buy.optionToBuy&id=2009-10283-008&CFID=2 3379563&CFTOKEN=78239404 and the opportunity to purchase the article for $11.95. Instead of providing the DOI, we would do this at the end (no period after the URL):

> Retrieved from http://psycnet.apa.org/index.cfm?fa=buy
> .optionToBuy&id=2009-10283-008&CFID=23379563&
> CFTOKEN=78239404

Try not to break a URL at the end of a line, but if you must, do so before a punctuation mark. Do not put a period at the end—that may cause the reader to include it in the retrieval and then it won't work.

Worst case: You want to cite a website that has no author, no year, no page numbers. See http://www.apastyle.org/learn/faqs/cite -website-material.aspx and hope for the best. Notice that what we just did is also the way to cite an entire website rather than an article: give the address in the text and put no entry in the references list.

Capitalization rules for URLs are as follows: Everything up to and including the host name (www.apastyle.org in the preceding example) is in lowercase. The rest must match exactly what you found on the web.

Exercise 5

Go to the website for the Institute for the Advancement of Social Work Research (http://www.iaswresearch.org) and search for a document you like. Cite it here:

_____

_____

Historical and Archival References

In qualitative research, it is possible that you will use personal interviewing as a method of collecting data because the participants are more comfortable talking than they are writing a response, as is often the case with aboriginal populations and immigrant groups, for example. Personal interview techniques include ethnographic interviews, conversations with historically informed participants, oral stories, and narrative histories. These methods help to inform the researcher about past values and norms, the culture and people of a particular group, the reconstruction of an experience, and information about dying lifestyles that help the researcher to interpret the past. Typically obtained from first-person accounts, this type of non-print source requires a different reference format than that of a personal communication notation in the text. The interviewee is listed as the author in the case of interviews and oral histories. Electronic databases (ERIC or JSTOR) can be used to locate some documents through a home page or URL page for an online archive.

Here is an example of a general interview format:

> Big Eagle, A. (Elder). (2006, January 19). Interview by M.J. Carlisle [Audio recording]. Northern Plains Women Artists Oral History Project. University of Alice Springs Aboriginal Archives (provide catalogue number).

Here is an example of an interview retrieved from the Internet:

> Big Eagle, A. (Elder). (2006, January 19). Interview by M.J. Carlisle [Audio recording]. Northern Plains Women Artists Oral History Project. University of Alice Springs Aboriginal Archives. Retrieved from http://www.uas.edu /NPWAOHP/bigeahle.html

Include the following elements for a general format, based on APA Style for archival materials.

- Author of the document (if known)

- Date it was created (if known)

- A title if it is available

- A description of the material (e.g., letter, speech, minutes of a meeting)

■ Name of the collection

■ As much information as needed to help locate the item with reasonable ease within the repository

■ Name and location of the repository

■ Note that brackets are used for information that is not part of the document itself

For example, a reference to a letter from an archival collection would be listed as follows:

> Tedious, I. M. (1925, May 5). [Letter to Emily Carr]. I. M. Tedious Papers, Harvard University Archives, Cambridge, MA.

References in the Body of the Manuscript

Citations in the text contain two parts: the author(s) and the year of publication. In the text, your citation would look like this:

> Szuchman and Thomlison (2006) validated the first measure of . . .

> In 2006, Szuchman and Thomlison validated the first measure of . . .

> The findings on childhood suicide (Szuchman & Thomlison, 2006) . . .

As was noted in Chapter 3, the last is usually preferred. The authors' names are typically not relevant to the point you are making, and if they are not directly relevant, then they are parenthetical.

When you are quoting from a source, use double quotation marks. Single quotation marks are used only when the author you are quoting is quoting someone else. In that case, the source contains double quotation marks, and these become single quotation marks in your manuscript. Final punctuation goes inside the quotation marks unless the quotation is followed by a page number in parentheses. When your quotation contains 40 or more words, use block form. That means that instead of using quotation marks, place the entire quotation in indented form. Indent one half inch from the left margin (in line with the start of paragraphs) and keep every line of the quotation indented just the same amount. Do not change the right margin; use the same right margin as the rest of your manuscript. The entire quotation is double-spaced.

You will have to cite the page number of the source for direct quotations. Do so after the closing quotation mark and before the period:

> Thomlison and Szuchman (2007) reported "Blah blah blah" (p. 23).

> If you want the authors' names in parentheses, do it like this:

> "Blah blah blah" (Thomlison & Szuchman, 2007, p. 23).

> When this occurs after a block quote, it comes in after the final punctuation:

> Mary had a little lamb, whose fleece was white as snow. Everywhere that Mary went, the lamb was sure to go. He followed her to school one day, which was against the rule. It made the children laugh and play to see a lamb at school. (p. 23)

The use of frequent quotations and long quotations is distracting; they do not belong in your paper.

Page references for online sources that are not paginated can be challenging. If paragraphs are numbered, use that number (e.g., para. 3). If they are not, use headings as locators (e.g., Explicit Communication section).

Here are some final quirks of APA referencing rules in your paper:

- Use the ampersand in parentheses and the word *and* in the text. It was a nice day (Corcoran & Thomlison, 2010). Corcoran and Thomlison (2010) found that people enjoy nice days.

- Use commas only for three or more authors even though you use a comma for only two authors in the References section.

> Cloudy, J. P., & Sunshine, I. (2008). Sure has been nice weather lately: Extra good news. *Journal of Weather, 7,* 12–30.

> Many people go fishing when the weather is fine (Cloudy & Sunshine, 2008).

> Some disagree with that view (Sleet, Hail, Snow, & Rain, 2009).

▩ When the work has two authors, always use both names (Szuchman & Thomlison, 2007).

▩ When the reference has more than two and fewer than six authors, name them all the first time you cite them (Thomlison, Cooper, Slipper, Becker, & Corcoran, 2005). In future citations in the text, name only the first and use *et al.* instead of the rest of the names on the list (Thomlison et al., 2005). When the work has six or more authors, use *et al.* after the first author's name even in the first reference.

▩ If you are referring to more than one article inside the same parentheses, use a comma to separate two items by the same author(s) and a semicolon to separate between authors. List them in the same order in which they would appear in the References section. Here is an example: This hypothesis has robust support (Szuchman, 1996; Thomlison & Becker, 1998; Turner et al., 1995).

▩ With groups as authors, cite the group the first time: (National Institute of Health [NIH], 2010). It is understood that the abbreviation followed by the publication year is acceptable in further citations. For example: The NIH (1997) studied substance abuse assessment profiles of Cuban adolescents.

Referencing the DSM

This is a book that is referenced all the time, and all of the rules for this situation are given at a website designed to teach you only about this one reference: http://supp.apa.org/style/pubman-ch07.02 .pdf—and watch out because a revision of that book is on the way. Meanwhile, at the time of this writing, you are citing the *Diagnostic and statistical manual of mental disorders* (4th ed., text rev.; *DSM-IV-TR*, American Psychiatric Association, 2000). The next time you mention it in your paper you just call it *DSM-IV-TR* (2000). There is an online edition as well, and if you use it you should also provide the DOI. In the References section it looks like this:

American Psychiatric Association. (2000). *Diagnostic and statistical manual of mental disorders* (4th ed., text rev.). Washington, DC: Author.

Looking Back and Looking Ahead

APA referencing style probably turned out to be less complicated than you might have thought, but as they say, the devil is in the details. You must follow the format exactly. The most striking difference between this referencing style and some others is that it contains only the works cited (although it does not have that name). Be sure to check that you have listed all the authors you have cited and that you have cited all the ones you have listed. Double-check the spelling of authors' names, and work to make the references very accurate. Then check to make sure they conform to the style: authors' last names and initials, capitalization of only first word in article titles, commas in the right places, ampersands (&) as needed, italics for journal and book titles. Most important, look up the rules when you are not sure, and don't assume that you know the rules.

In the next chapter, you will learn how the first page of your manuscript should look and how to work with the settings on your word processor to conform to the final set of details.

For more information:

Topic	Publication Manual	Concise Rules
Accurate and complete reference list	6.22	7.23
Spaces after periods	4.01	2.01
Reference citations in text	6.11–6.31	7.12–7.22
Hanging indent	2.11	—
Alphabetizing	6.25	7.26
Author and editor information	6.27	7.28
Publication date	6.28	7.29
Title	6.29	7.30
Journal information	6.30	7.31
Book publisher information	6.31	7.31
Publishers' locations/postal abbreviations	6.30	7.31
Examples: periodicals	7.01	8.01
Examples: books and book chapters	7.02	8.02

(table continues)

Topic	Publication Manual	Concise Rules
Electronic sources	6.31–6.32 http://www .apastyle.org/learn/faqs /cite-website-material .aspx	7.32–7.33
Citing an entire website	http://www.apastyle .org/learn/faqs /cite-website.aspx	
Capitalization rules for URLs	6.31	7.32
Archival documents and interviews	7.10	8.10
Referencing *DSM*	http://supp.apa.org /style/pubman-ch07.02 .pdf	

12

Preparing the Title Page and Formatting Your Manuscript

Many people write with a working title in their minds but find that the finished product is actually an imperfect match for the title originally proposed. The title is very important, and careful thought should be given to preparing a succinct and, preferably, interesting title. Students working on course assignments often use the title of the course as listed in the syllabus for the paper or research report, but that is an inappropriate title for the paper. It is common for both professionals and students to compose the final title after the manuscript is written.

Like any title page, the title page of your APA-style manuscript contains the title of your paper, your name, and other identifying data. In addition, it contains information unique to APA style that is intended for the convenience of the editor and the printer of the journal to which the article may be submitted: the manuscript page heading and the running head. The difficulties students have involve (a) composing a good title and (b) understanding the difference between the manuscript page heading and the running head.

Writing a Title

The *Publication Manual* directs that titles *should*

1. Be 12 words or fewer.

2. Make sense standing alone.

3. Name the important variables or theoretical issues.

4. Identify the relationships among variables.

A title *should not*

1. Contain abbreviations.

2. Waste words (like *A Study of*).

3. Be witty or cute.

It is no wonder that students need practice in writing titles that conform to all these requirements. Often after accounting for variables and being sure to make sense, authors find themselves with very long first-try titles. Nevertheless, that is a good way to begin.

Write everything you think you need without worrying about length. At this point, it helps to think of the problem as a word puzzle; very often word puzzles can be fun. First, get rid of anything unnecessary, such as "A Study of" or "An Investigation of." The title "An Investigation of the Relationship Between Hat Sizes and Performance in Undergraduate Research Methods Classes" would benefit from that kind of cleanup.

Now you might find yourself with a title that starts with the words "The Relationship Between" or "The Effect of." Even though this is acceptable according to the *Publication Manual,* it is not the best way to start. First, it is likely that you can save words if you find another way to convey this idea. Second, it is wise to begin with a word of specific importance to your study, because when researchers glance through a list of titles in order to decide what to read, their attention is captured best by the first word. Can you phrase the title in the form of a question? This is often a good alternative: "Do Undergraduate and Graduate Social Work Students Wear Special Styles of Hats?" Choose your first word or phrase so that it applies uniquely to your own study. Some examples are "Child and Family Characteristics Associated with Outcomes in Foster Care," "Social Security Reduction Effects on Older Adults," "Development of an Instrument to Measure Restrictiveness," and "A Controlled Evaluation of Service to Reduce Teen Pregnancy." Create titles that begin with important variables.

Create titles that begin with important variables.

 # Exercise 1

It is worthwhile to look at some creative approaches to this "effect of" problem and work backward. Copy some titles that start with key words, and indicate how they would be written if the author had written a lazy "effect of" title instead:

1. Sometimes authors start with a catchy research question and then move on to the variables. "Does Violence Beget Violence? The Relationship Between Adolescents' Violent Behaviors and Parental Disciplinary Practices." This is better than "The Effect of Parental Disciplinary Practices on Adolescents' Violent Behaviors."

2. Sometimes authors put variables up front. "Gender and Ethnicity: Effects on Service Utilization."

3. "Gender and Racial Discrimination Behaviors." This works better than "Effect of Gender on Racial Discrimination Behaviors."

4. _____

    _____

5. _____

    _____

6. _____

    _____

In scanning titles for Exercise 1, you undoubtedly noticed many that began with "The Effect of." You also saw some alternatives, and three probably stand out: the question title, the colon title, and the "and" title. The question title ("Does Violence Beget Violence?") works because it is attention grabbing. The colon title works because it allows important variables (gender and ethnicity) to be identified before the words *effect* or *relationship* are used (but these words can still be used for clarity). The "and" title names the variables, uses "and" between them, and depends on the reader to infer which is the dependent and which is the independent variable. If you use an "and" title, be sure there is little likelihood that a reader could make the wrong inference. In this case, "Gender and Racial Discrimination Behaviors" is just as informative as "Racial Discrimination Behaviors and Gender."

Elements of the Title Page

Now that your title is written, you have only to follow some rules about getting it on a title page.

1. Type the title centered on the page. Capitalize important words. Do not capitalize every letter. Do not use a font different from what is in the body of the paper and do not use bold type. If you use two lines because your title cannot fit on one line, double-space between them and break the title at a meaningful point, not whenever the line is full.

2. Center your name one double space below the title. Decide today what your professional name will be. Most people use a first name and middle initial. Of course, some people have names that are more complex than others, with two middle names or a hyphenated last name. Decide how it should look, but do not stray far from the first name–middle initial–last name approach. Your name might change between your first publication and your last, but you should not change your professional name if you want people to know who you are. Again, use uppercase and lowercase letters, nothing fancy. Do not use the word *by*.

3. Center the name of your institution one double space below your name.

4. Your instructor might want additional information, such as course number and date. If you have no specific instructions, just stop with name and institutional affiliation.

5. Decide on a running head of 50 characters (letters, spaces, and punctuation all count). The running head is a short version of your title that makes sense. If your title itself

contains fewer than 50 characters, use the whole title. The running head is what would be used as the page header in the actual printed journal and what readers use to find their place or remember what they are reading. This running head is placed on all your pages flush left near the top. On the title page, type the words *Running head* followed by a colon. Then type your running head in all uppercase letters. Here is an example:

Running head: TABLE MANNERS FOR PRIMATES

6. Create a manuscript page header. First go to the Format Page command. Choose the option that allows a different header for the first page. Use the "header" command on your word processor to create a flush right header for the title page. The header contains the running head (along with the words (*Running head*) just as it looks in #5 above. Prepare the header so that the running head is flush left, and a page number is flush right. Make sure the font matches the rest of your paper (Times New Roman 12-point). This is what your header looks like for the title page.

Running head: TABLE MANNERS FOR PRIMATES   1

Then on the next page, repeat the process but remove the words *Running head*. The actual running head is flush left, and the page number is on the far right. Example:

TABLE MANNERS FOR PRIMATES   2

 **Exercise 2**

Copy some running heads (look in the *upper margin*s of journal articles) and the titles of the articles to which they refer.

1. Running head: GRANDPARENTS REARING GRANDCHILDREN
    Title: Evaluating the Effectiveness of Biological Support Services to Grandparents Rearing Grandchildren.

2. _____

    _____

3. _____

_____

4. _____

_____

Formatting

By the time you prepare your title page, you _are probably_ just about finished with your paper. Follow all of the general formatting rules for your paper. Here are a few things students sometimes forget.

1. Use Times New Roman 12-point font. You may use Arial or Helvetica in preparing graphs.

2. If you use special characters (e.g., Greek letters, multiplication signs for interactions), use the ones in your word processor ("insert symbol"). Don't just make it up (like using X instead of the symbol for chi, χ.)

3. Start a new page after the abstract, for the references, and for each table and figure. Do not start any other sections with a new page.

4. Double-space everything. The only exception is that you may use single spacing or 1.5 spacing for tables.

5. Use at least a 1-inch margin on all sides. Your word processor's default setting should work fine for this.

6. Do not allow your word processor to right- or full-justify your lines. The right margin should be "ragged." Look for an "alignment" command and choose "left." That way, you will get a straight left margin and a rough one on the right.

7. Do not allow your word processor to hyphenate at the ends of lines. This will probably mean changing the default settings. Try locating "line and page breaks" somewhere in the paragraph or document menu. Any hyphen that appears at the end of the line should be a "hard hyphen," one that belongs there whether it is the end of a line or not.

8. Use the tab function to set your paragraphs to indent ½ inch. But don't indent the abstract, certain headings that should be centered or flush left, figure captions, or items on your reference list (those should have a hanging indent).

9. The order of pages is

   Title page

   Abstract

   Body of the paper

   References

   Tables

   Figures

   Appendixes

10. Use one space after commas, colons, some periods except

    ▪ No space within abbreviations (e.g., U.S., i.e.)

    ▪ Two spaces at the end of a sentence

11. Use your spelling-checker wisely. It can help you to spell words correctly if the word you have typed does not exist. It will not help you if you type *there* instead of *their*. Use your spelling-checker, and then use your brain.

Do not begin the Method, Results, or Discussion sections on a new page. Double-space throughout. The right margin should not be justified. Do not hyphenate at the ends of lines except when a hyphen is required as part of the spelling of the word.

Looking Back and Looking Ahead

In this chapter, you have noticed how difficult it is to create a title that is just right: It is concise, it differentiates your study from others with similar variables, it creates anticipation, and it identifies the important variables and relationships. You also learned that the title appears on a title page with five distinct elements: the title, your name, your affiliation, a running head, and a page header. Presenting a paper with this title page to a journal editor or an instructor is a way of saying that you are in the club, that you know the rules of writing in your profession. The reader will approach your work with a positive, optimistic attitude.

You are now also aware of the other formatting rules for APA papers: the margins, the common font types, the spacing. Pay attention to the need to turn off automatic end-of-line hyphenation and to eliminate the justification of the right margin. These are other simple ways to look smart.

Now you have had practice with all the parts of your manuscript. So what can be left to do? Check Chapter 13 for some hints on polishing the paper by revising and proofreading.

For more information:

Topic	Publication Manual	Concise Rules
Choosing a title	2.01	—
Author's name and affiliation	2.02	—
Elements of Title page	8.03	—
Running head	8.03	—
Font	8.03	—
Double-spacing	8.03	—
Margins	8.03	—
Justification, hyphen	8.03	—
Order of sections/parts	8.03	—
Page numbers and headers	8.03	—
Paragraphs and indentation	8.03	—
Spacing after punctuation	4.01, 4.40	2.01, 4.10

13
Polishing the Paper

You are probably not surprised to learn that after writing the first draft of your paper, you still have work to do. But the worst is over, so give yourself a moment to enjoy that feeling. We have named this chapter "Polishing the Paper" because the phrase has two meanings. Think of the rewriting and editing you do after the first draft in two ways: (1) You will now finish up your project, and (2) you will do what is necessary to make it shine.

Students sometimes call this *proofreading,* but that is not the correct word. It makes it sound as though after your first draft, all you have to do is check it over for typing and spelling errors. That is what you do with the last draft, which is a bit further down the line. Polishing the paper comprises three steps: *First, you revise; second, you edit; third, you proofread.* Each of these steps may involve more than one draft.

Step 1: Rewrite and Revise

The first rewrite (resulting in the second draft) must be conceptual. This will be a long process, so save a day to do it. The best approach is to finish your first draft two full days before it is due (assuming that you can devote a big part of those two days to this paper—otherwise, allow extra days). In this rewrite, you will not give APA style a thought. You are revising the paper so that it is well organized and flows logically.

Introduction

Think through the sequencing of your paragraphs. Try to remember what your purpose was for each one, and review the order to see whether it is correct. Check to make sure that you have included all the following pieces of your argument in the proper places:

- The purpose of your study
- Why it is important
- Hypotheses or research questions
- Rationales for hypotheses
- General information about method
- Definitions of variables

Look for paragraphs with only one or two sentences. If you find any, fix them now. Elaborate on what you have written, move the material to a more logical place, or remove those sentences.

Now try to outline your introduction. Outline what is really there, not what you meant to write. Step back and see whether that outline is the best possible organization of your material. If you see whole paragraphs in the wrong place, move them. After they have been moved, make sure the transitions still work. Change them if they do not. If you see gaps where something should be explained or fleshed out, do it.

Check your subheadings. See whether they still work now that you have made some changes. Can you improve on them? If you have not used subheadings, consider putting some in now.

Method and Procedure

First, look over your subheadings and make sure they accurately describe the material in each section. Next, examine the information you provide about participants. Check to be sure that you have reported the essentials:

- Age and gender
- Type of population participants represent (e.g., first-year social work students)
- Compensation they received for participating
- How many did not complete the study and why
- Appropriate demographic information for each group (if applicable)

If you used a measure, check to be sure that you have

- Provided enough information for replication
- Made clear the experience participants had using it
- Provided the name and author, and indicate how readers could obtain it

If you have a special section for description of measures, does it stand alone or does it depend on information about conditions? If it makes no sense to someone who is unfamiliar with your conditions, reorganize now. If you have used materials created by you, such as a special log or journal book for the participants, check that you have included the appropriate information describing the process used to develop and establish the instrument for others to replicate.

Be sure you have provided all the steps in the process. What was kept in the measure and what was deleted during the development process? Have you provided examples? Is there enough information to replicate?

Look at the *procedure*. Try very hard to put yourself in the shoes of someone who was not there. Are there any sentences that would not make sense for that person? If so, they are not necessarily bad sentences; more likely, they are in the wrong place. The best thing would be to try this section out on a friend. As you read it aloud, watch that person's face. If you notice a puzzled look, you have skipped some information that your audience needs in order to put the pieces together clearly. Alternatively, have the friend read the section aloud to you.

Check to be sure that you have

- Done a good job conveying the instructions that you gave to participants
- Provided enough information to replicate
- Included instructions on scoring (if applicable)

Results

Look at your original data analysis. Make sure that every analysis that should be in your paper is there. Double-check *every* number against the printout from the statistics package you used or against the calculation that you did. This is also a good time to make sure that letters used in reporting statistics (e.g., t, n, F, p) are italicized (but not the Greek letters).

If you have used tables or figures to display data, each of them should be mentioned in this section. There should be enough information in the text to allow the reader to know what types of data are in the tables and figures. Also, the relevant means and percentages should be either in the text or in tables (or figures), not in both places.

Discussion

With your introduction on one side and your discussion on the other, check that every hypothesis or question mentioned in one is mentioned in the other. Then do the same thing with your results on one side and your discussion on the other.

Now outline your Discussion section. If you have only topics and no subtopics in your outline, you may have restated your results without discussing them. Remember your options:

- Similarities between your findings and someone else's
- Differences between your findings and someone else's
- Relationship between these findings and theories mentioned in the introduction
- Alternative explanations for the findings
- Suggested explanations for negative results
- Limitations of the study
- Implications of the findings
- Practical applications
- Suggestions for further research (with rationales)

References

This is a good time to check your references. Every reference in your paper should be on your references list and vice versa. Check the spellings while you are at it; your spelling-checker will not pick up errors in people's names. It is important to check that the year reported in the text is the same as the year in the references. This is a common source of error, and it is time consuming to resolve.

Abstract

The last part of the first rewrite is checking the abstract. Assuming that you worked hard to get it right the first time, at this point, you have only to double-check to make sure that any changes you made in the body of the paper do not affect the abstract. If you are still pleased with it, move on to the next step of polishing your paper.

Step 2: Edit and Rewrite

With your major revisions behind you, it is time to concentrate on organization and style. You are probably tired of the paper by now, but that is to be expected. You will learn to love this paper again before you hand it in because it will be so polished.

Begin with the paragraphs. Does each one start with a topic sentence? Does something about that sentence make clear why the paragraph is located where it is? For example, is there a subheading nearby that makes the reader expect such a topic? Is there a transition word that relates to the previous paragraph? Remember, you have a list in Chapter 3—use it. Finally, does every sentence in that paragraph relate to the topic? Now you have to check every sentence for gross errors. First, make sure that each sentence is really a sentence, not a run-on or a fragment. Next, find the grammatical subject of every sentence and underline it. Then, make sure the verb is appropriate in number. While you are at it, make sure that the verb defines an action that is logically possible for the subject. For example, if you have written that a study *tried* to do something, now is the time to reconsider. Think about misplaced modifiers at this time. Admittedly, misplaced modifiers are not always easy to spot in your own work, but sometimes when you are studying your sentences this closely, you can spot them.

This is also the time to check for errors in parallel construction. These, too, can be hard to spot; look especially at items in a series, at compound verbs, and at phrases containing comparisons. You are in the stage of finalizing your paper now. Perfection is near—we hope.

Step 3: Proofread (Not a Rewrite)

You are nearing the home stretch, preparing to put a shine on that paper. Pass your eyes over your paper again. You may even read it aloud which can provide a different perspective from a silent read. Circle the commas and colons. Try to remind yourself of the actual rule you learned in school or in this book that prescribes that punctuation mark in that place. You should have a grammar book somewhere on your desk; perhaps you can find that rule. If you cannot specify the rule, you should seriously consider omitting the punctuation mark. Most of what is left can be streamlined with the use of the search function on your word processor. If you are not yet familiar with this function, take some time now to figure out how to *find* or *search* for a word or phrase. Also, it is a good idea to figure out the command that takes you to the top of your document because it will be efficient to return there after each search.

When you are ready, search for and correct the following, if necessary:

- *Apostrophe:* For each one, if it is used in a contraction, change the contraction to a more formal phrase. If it is a simple plural with no possession intended, omit the apostrophe. If the intention is possessive but the word is a pronoun, omit the apostrophe. If it is a possessive noun, note whether it is singular or plural and make sure the apostrophe is in the right place.

- *Their:* First, make sure you did not mean to write *there*. When that is taken care of, check that the noun referred to is apparent to the reader and that it is plural. Then do a search for *there* just to make sure you didn't mean to write *their*.

- *Feel, felt, think, thought, believe, believed, say, said, state, stated, prove,* and *proved:* If these refer to the activities of researchers you have cited, think it over. Perhaps you should substitute one of the words from your list of researcher verbs in Chapter 3.

- *Current* and *present:* Do not use these words to refer to studies other than yours.

- Data, hypotheses, hypothesis, stimulus, stimuli, analysis, analyses, phenomena, phenomenon, criteria, and criterion: There is always a danger that the verbs in these sentences might not agree in number with these nouns.

- *Since* and *while:* Remember, the *Publication Manual* specifies that these words are used only in their temporal sense. You might need to substitute *because* and *whereas* if they are more accurate.

- *Between* and *among:* Use *between* for two things, *among* for more than two.

- *You* and *we:* Unless you are quoting instructions to participants, rephrase without these words.

- *Non, pre, post,* and *sub:* These are not words. They have to be attached to other words.

- &: *Ampersands* should appear only in parentheses. Authors' names are joined by *and* outside parentheses.

- *Latin abbreviations:* Make sure that they are punctuated correctly and that they appear only in parentheses except when *et al.* is used in a citation (Smith et al., 1998).

Now you can run your spelling-checker. It will not help you with names, so look them over each time the spelling-checker finds them. Check the spelling yourself.

Final Touches

You have only one task left. Read your paper aloud. Read every word you have written. This is how you will notice whether you have left little words out or put extra ones in. All writers have trouble seeing dumb little mistakes because we know what something is supposed to say. Cognitive psychologists call this *top-down processing*; our minds are working with meaning, so sometimes our eyes miss the details.

This is the time when you begin to feel proud of your work; you are not feeling as sick of it as you were by the second revision. This is because you can appreciate how many little improvements you made even after you thought you were finished. You can finally take this paper out in public (or hand it in to your professor), and it will surely make a good impression.

Looking Back and Looking Ahead

You have learned the difference between revising and proofreading. You know now that revising is time consuming, and you will plan to allow sufficient time for this work before presenting the final written draft. However, other presentation formats are also used by professionals in social work. For those fortunate readers who are asked to present their research in a public forum, the next chapter provides some guidance for the preparation of posters and PowerPoint presentations.

14

Preparing a Presentation

Many students are required to prepare a presentation, report or a review paper in the style of an APA manuscript for at least one social work class. However, because your first professional presentation is likely to be in the form of a poster presentation, it is helpful to practice this format in either the research methods class or practice methods class to learn the guidelines for preparing a professional poster paper. There are also several regional (National Association of Social Workers) and national (Society for Social Work and Research and the Council on Social Work Education Annual Meeting) social work conferences and annual meetings every year that feature poster papers with sections for student presentations. Poster presentations are a particularly interesting method of conveying information visually. Preparing a poster paper for a conference is a good way to participate in professional forums if you do not feel ready to present an oral paper.

Poster Presentations

What Is a Poster Session?

Conferences or professional meetings often make poster sessions available for presenters to display an overview of their research or study on a board measuring about 4 by 6 feet. All of the data appear on this large sheet. Posters are arranged in rows, filling the room reserved for this purpose where many authors display their work at the same time. Oral papers may be presented in other rooms at the conference during the time poster sessions are provided as an option for conference attendees to learn about scientific results. A time and location number for the poster to be displayed is given to the presenter who arrives at the appointed time to pin the poster to the board and accompany the display. Interested people can walk by, read the information, and discuss the findings and the project with the presenter. This goes on for 1 to 2 hours. At some conferences, the posters will remain during the entire conference. At others, posters will change during the conference to enable many people to present.

Posters always include a presentation of data from a research study or topical review. Posters of research studies usually present data from a large body of data with careful attention to the presentation of the research design and data analysis. A poster is also an effective way to present the results from smaller studies, such as work with a child, a single-subject design study, small-group designs, or other intervention elements of special visual interest. Posters of topical reviews usually present the theoretical framework, the key concepts, the literature search method, and the synthesized and organized results of the review.

Presenting a poster has advantages over presenting a talk. For one thing, it is less frightening. For another, only people who really have an interest in your work are paying attention, and you have their full attention. You might come away with ideas for improvement for the next study or ways in which the current data could be better presented. Observers can ask questions and spend as little or as much time with a presentation as they want. The disadvantage is that it requires some serious planning to make the presentation as reader friendly as possible in this type of situation. People will be on their feet, they will be distracted by a lot of ambient noise, and they will be unsure about how much time to commit to any given poster in light of what remains to be seen. Developing strong empathy for the consumer's plight will help you to decide what to present on your poster and how to display it.

Even though poster presentations are increasingly popular as methods of dissemination of research findings, the *Publication Manual* provides no guidance in preparing one. What, then, do authors rely on for poster rules? First, when a poster is accepted for presentation, presenters are usually provided with very brief guidelines from the organization sponsoring the conference. Know the conference guidelines before you start to design your poster. These generally include (1) the size of the display area each author will have; (2) the suggestion that the poster should be readable from a distance of about 3 feet (with the lettering for title, author, and affiliation at least 1 inch high and the rest at least 3.8 inches high); and (3) a diagram of possible arrangements of title, abstract, introduction, method, results, and conclusions.

Your poster must be readable from a distance of 3 feet.

Although these are useful guidelines, the second method for learning how to present your findings in poster format is even more effective: Go to a poster session. You will see that there are limitless ways to follow the general rules provided by the conference organizers, and you might even see that some people have ignored some rules completely but that other rules are generally followed. You will quickly learn, for example, that the rule about the font being legible from a distance is not a good one to break, because no one seems tempted to read the posters with small print. Students in or near major metropolitan areas might have the opportunity to attend a national or regional social work meeting that includes poster presentations. If your college, internship agency, or professional association has an annual forum of some type, make every effort to attend it. We sometimes organize a poster conference of students' master's theses and dissertation studies; this can be a great opportunity to experience what this sort of presentation entails.

You are not bound to APA style—only the spirit of the style. That means that you must be clear, fair to those whose work came before yours, and intellectually honest about the positive and negative sides of what you have done. But it also means that you do not need to follow a rigid format. You can use numbered lists or bulleted points instead of paragraphs, for example. You can use tables or circles and arrows to illustrate your theories or research design.

 Posters are true to the spirit of APA format, but the rules of presentation are relaxed.

Creating the Poster

Creating a poster that grabs the attention of many people will take planning and time. To begin, start planning your poster well in advance of the presentation date. We suggest that you allow three weeks to plan the poster, draft the text, tables, and charts; edit and proofread the poster before it is ready for public viewing or for the printer.

One major consideration in planning your poster is to know that posters have limited content. Too much detail may not be read. But how much information do you need to include? A poster will have more or less the same components of a research study. The required sections are the Title, Author(s) and Affiliation(s), Abstract, Background (introduction), Method, and Results sections. The source of funding should be included if the study had a sponsor. Other information or headings may be considered as well. Use the same abstract that you prepared for your written research report.

The introduction or background must be substantially shorter than it is in your research paper. Consider one or two sentences relevant to the background of the problem; include the purpose and significance of the topic and, of course, the hypotheses. Here are some ways to highlight relevant literature:

- Discuss the first study to address your topic in its current form. Then describe a very relevant recent one, especially if you are replicating and extending it. There might be more than one study very similar to yours; mention several of the most similar ones.

- Discuss the competing theoretical positions surrounding your work. Then describe the study that most resembles your method.

- Provide a general explanation, without references, about how this problem has been traditionally addressed in research. Then explain, with references if appropriate, how you will diverge from this tradition and why.

Keep the introduction as short as you can. Try to keep it to two or three pages of large type. Remember the distractions that the reader faces. In these situations, people might read only a part of what you have written. If there is a crucial section of the introduction that you want viewers to read, make it visually distinct from the rest. Do this with the tricks that your computer can produce, such as bullets, frames, bold italics, and color.

Make the Introduction section no longer than three largetype pages.

The Method section has the potential to attract the most attention. Here, you briefly describe your research method and/or summarize the interventions. Decide what is the most efficient way for someone to get the feeling of what the participants experienced. You might want to post the materials themselves (or portions of them). If you showed pictures, post the pictures. If participants read vignettes, put up a sample. If they performed a task with a piece of equipment, include a snapshot of someone using the equipment. If they made copies of drawings, put up a sample of the drawing and a sample copy. You do not have to provide the detail necessary to replicate the study; you have to provide the minimum necessary for someone to understand what you did. Of course, if you borrowed any of the details from a previous author, you will need to provide the references. In a brief narrative of the method, include enough to satisfy the observer that you did it right:

- The number of participants and any important data about them

- The research design

- A brief description of the procedures

- The grouping variables

- The nature of the control condition, if used

- The name(s) of the instruments used to measure the variables

 Consider posting parts or photos of the actual materials.

The results that you post will be primarily tables and figures. If possible, present the results in graphic form rather than in a table. Color helps to accentuate the findings in bar charts, graphs, and pie charts. Include easy-to-read titles and labels. You need only introduce them with a statement of the analyses you conducted and the significant findings.

Instead of a discussion section, posters usually have *conclusions*. The difference is that conclusions are less speculative and more directly tied to the hypotheses and results. There is no room for implications or suggestions for future research. Conclusions can be a few numbered points that you make about the relationship between the results and the hypotheses or research questions.

 Posters usually have conclusions, presented in bulleted or numbered highlights, in place of a discussion.

You will have to prepare the References section if you referred to others' work. Occasionally, you will see posters written without references, but students should plan on a brief list of references.

Set up PowerPoint to Create a Poster

Now it is time to compose the text using a program such as Power-Point and then print it to a single sheet with a large-format printer. You set up a single PowerPoint slide sized to match the requirements specified by the conference organizers (e.g., 24 × 36 in. or 36 × 48 in.). If you do not have the use of such a printer, you can find online or local business services that do the printing. It is costly but necessary.

The letters in the title should be about 1 inch tall, and the poster should be readable from about 3 feet. Choose a font size that will do this by working at 100% view in your word processor and trying out a few fonts. Then step back. Some fonts work well in boldface type throughout. Arial and Avant Garde are good choices for the title. Times Roman and Century Schoolbook are effective choices for the body of text. Others are already bold enough when printed in very large size. Section titles can be set apart by color and font size. Use dark text on a light background for maximum effectiveness. Avoid busy designs and dark ominous colors. Avoid underlining, and format the text flush left with a ragged right. Many people use their university logo somewhere on the poster. You can probably find one designed for sharing somewhere on your university's website. But don't feel compelled to do this. It's a matter of personal taste unless your university has a policy on it.

If you do not already know how, you need to learn how to manage text boxes for this task. You place each element of your presentation (e.g., the abstract) in its own text box and line them up—across or down—in a way that makes the flow obvious. You can use numbers or arrows if it is not obvious. Make the titles of these sections large and clear. Copy and paste the material from your word-processed draft. Keep it brief. Let there be lots of white space (50% of your poster should be blank). Keep the background light (white is preferable) rather than using a lot of color and texture in the background. There are many templates on the web that you can hunt through. They are not all excellent, however. And if you are purchasing the printing through an online service, many of them offer templates as well. Purrington (2009) has a great site at http://www.swarthmore.edu/NatSci/cpurrin1/posteradvice.htm—even though he is a biologist! (Some of his advice doesn't apply to you; for example, he suggests that a poster should not contain an abstract, but that is contrary to our cultural environment.) He also sponsors a "Pimp My Poster" group on Flickr: http://www.flickr.com/groups/688685@N24/ where people post their drafts and get advice. Here are two additional sites with templates that we found in an Internet search:

> www.sacs.ucsf.edu/Newsletters/Templates/36x48_horiz_template.ppt

> http://groups.ucanr.org/posters/Templates_for_Posters/

The second one has a nice example of scientific style—see if you can locate it among the various other examples provided for other purposes on that website.

The take-home message for posters is that they need to be attractive enough for someone to pause and read, easy enough to read and understand in a noisy, busy environment (sometimes even with a cash bar nearby), and assembled in a way that puts science ahead of everything else.

Finally, print a copy of the poster on your own printer. Use the "scale fit to paper" command. You'll get a good idea of the clarity of your presentation. If you can't read it without a magnifying glass, your font is too small. You will be able to use this reduced version as a handout at the conference. Make sure that your email address is on the poster, and if it is too small to be legible on the handout, prepare a version with an enlarged email address just for the handout. The last test is to ask a friend to stand 3 feet back from your poster and help you to decide if it is easy to read.

Conference organizers often suggest how many handouts to prepare. If this is an in-house function, your instructor will guide you. People who browse posters expect to have a hard copy available to take home for future reference. If you are using a manuscript format for the handout rather than a reduced version of the poster, be sure to include your address and email address on the title page as people may want to contact you after the conference; sometimes they do just that.

Preparing Yourself

What will actually happen at the poster session is that strangers will walk up to your poster, give it a glance, and do one of three things:

1. Walk away

2. Read it

3. Talk to you

If it is the first, you will feel rejected. No one can adequately prepare for that. If it is the second, you will wonder what to do with yourself while this happens. Again, until it happens, you cannot know how to prepare. You might ask whether they would like to know more or whether they have any questions you can answer. But if it is the third, you can be prepared. That is because people always say approximately the same thing: "Tell me the quick version of what you did." You went to all the trouble of making it artistic, easy to read, and self-standing. Yet this stranger wants you to tell it? Shocking! But you can be ready. Go for the visual space that you designed to stand out; point to it, and give your already prepared quick oral version. If this is an in-house event such as a classroom poster presentation, you might feel less anxious. If this is a professional meeting for social workers, prepare for the audience.

Finally, here is advice from our own research methods classes. After the students presented posters for the first time, we asked for the single most important piece of advice that they would give to next year's class. Their answer? Eat lunch first and wear comfortable shoes!

Oral Presentations

PowerPoint presentation software is a good organizing tool for public speaking. However, students and professionals have been known to overuse some of its features. If you are preparing to present your research to a group—in a class, your internship setting, or at a conference—remember that the most important object in the room is you, not the screen. People should be involved with what you are saying, not with what you have on a board behind you. A few simple rules will help you to arrange that.

About You

- Practice. Try to be able to speak without looking at notes. Have them in your hand or on the podium, but just so that you will sleep better the night before, not so that you can be less prepared when the time comes.

- Know when to change slides and know how to do it on the equipment you will have. Get there early enough to understand how the machines in that room work.

- Be prepared for equipment failure. Be able to talk without the slides.

- Dress professionally. If your classroom attire is casual, kick it up a notch on the day of your talk. Notice that at a conference, the speakers are usually dressed more professionally than many in the audience.

- Look at the audience and not at the screen with your slides. Do not read your presentation from the screen. To make eye contact, you have to be looking at something with eyes. So does your audience.

The Content of Your Slides

Use the slides to outline your talk. Use key phrases about your topic and isolated words onscreen, and elaborate in your talk on the basis of what is on the screen. Avoid using too much text on the slide. Never put complete sentences on your slides so that you will not be tempted to read your slides. You can put material on slides that is important but boring, such as the demographic data on your participants. A slide can show the total number, their gender breakdown, and their ages, and you can say something different—more interesting— about them (perhaps that they were all prisoners or all single parents) and then just stand for a moment so that your audience can take in the numbers on the screen.

Strive for clarity of form and content. Use simple fonts and make them bold. Use the same font consistently throughout the presentation. Remember that less is more; make only a few points with each slide. Most people recommend no more than six lines of text and no more than six words per line. Another common general rule is that a 20-minute presentation should have no more than 20 slides.

You can cite references, but just the author and year. It is not necessary to put the full reference on your slide. People will find the source if they need it. Do not read the year of publication aloud. Finally, do not put up a reference list at the end.

Tables and graphs are very welcome. But do not read the numbers. Discuss the trends. For example, you can put a means table up, and without reading the numbers, you can indicate which means were significantly different. You can put up a correlation table and call attention to significant relationships, again without stating numbers that are there for all to see. For graphs, make sure the labels are large enough for the audience to read.

If you use a graph, refer to the colors to describe the trends:

The red bars reflect the time spent on homework, and the blue bars reflect time spent in paid employment. The first pair of bars represents the athletes, and the second pair represents the cheerleaders. As you see, both groups spent little time in paid employment (and that small difference on the graph is not significant), but the cheerleaders spent much more time watching television.

After describing your method (some sample items from measures would be welcome on screen), you can combine talk of hypotheses, results, and discussion. That is, you can say that you expected a certain outcome. Then show the graph or table that resulted. Briefly mention a few interesting things about it. Then move on to your next hypothesis. Nothing will be lost if you fail to use headings for results and discussion.

Another thing that you can do is work with symbols. Any symbolic representations of your data or your ideas will also enhance your posters, by the way.

Here are some examples:

Use horizontal arrows when you want to imply time sequence or causation:

Ice cream cones to participants	$\rightarrow$	higher return rate for questionnaires
Electric shock	$\rightarrow$	lower return rate

Use vertical arrows for *up* and *down*, for example when you want to say which groups improved and which did not:

Depression: older adults $\uparrow$ younger adults $\downarrow$

Anxiety: older adults $\uparrow$ younger adults $\downarrow$

Life satisfaction: older adults $\uparrow$ younger adults $\uparrow$

Use greater than (>) or less than (<) or equal (=) signs to show group differences:

Hypothesis 1: depression

   older adults > younger adults

Hypothesis 2: life satisfaction

   older adults < younger adults

Avoid Distracting Effects

Avoid the following distractions:

- Images that are decorative rather than explanatory
- Weird fonts (Arial and Verdana are always safe)
- Small fonts
- Fonts that change from slide to slide
- Animation and flying text
- Text moving in from different places for each slide
- Too many colors

■ Annoying color contrast—use high contrasting colors (a safe choice would be a white or very light background with a black or blue font)

■ Busy backgrounds

■ Backgrounds that change from slide to slide

Looking Back and Looking Ahead

In addition to presenting your work in written format, you are now prepared to make a poster presentation or an oral presentation. Often, the poster presentation is done as a first step in making your findings public. It is easy to submit to a conference if you have good data; the rules for submission generally require a short summary. If you are submitting a poster, you just need to prepare the broad outlines and a few details. While you are attending your poster presentation, you may get some good ideas for further analysis or further research.

At many conferences, the oral presentations are reserved for more complete projects, and they are often part of a group of presentations on a similar topic—a symposium. The symposium is the conference submission, and if it is accepted, all of the talks are accepted as a package. However, students are often required to practice all the formats for presenting research.

Now that you have come to the end of this chapter, you are really ready to show off your skills, no matter what the venue.

References

American Psychological Association. (2010). *Concise rules of APA style* (6th ed.). Washington, DC: Author.

American Psychological Association. (2010). *Publication manual of the American Psychological Association* (6th ed.). Washington, DC: Author.

Bem, D. J. (1995). Writing a review article for *Psychological Bulletin*. *Psychological Bulletin, 118*, 172–177.

Liddle, H. A., Jackson-Gilfort, A., & Marvel, F. A. (2006). An empirically supported and culturally specific engagement and intervention strategy for African American adolescent males. *American Journal of Orthopsychiatry, 76*, 215–225.

Mendelsohn, H. N. (1997). *An author's guide to social work journals* (4th ed.). Washington, DC: NASW Press.

National Association of Social Workers. (2008). *Code of ethics of the National Association of Social Workers*, Revised by the 2008 NASW Delegate Assembly. Retrieved July 26, 2009, from http://www .socialworkers.org/pubs/code/default.asp

Nicol, A. A. M., & Pexman, P. M. (1999). *Presenting your findings: A practical guide for creating tables*. Washington, DC: American Psychological Association.

Nicol, A. A. M., & Pexman, P. M. (2003). *Displaying your findings: A practical guide for creating figures, posters, and presentations*. Washington, DC: American Psychological Association.

Rimer, S. (2003, September 3). A campus fad that's being copied: Internet plagiarism seems on the rise. [Internet version]. Retrieved on January 28, 2007, from http://select.nytimes.com/search/restricted/article?res =F60F10F9395C0C708CDDA00894DB404482

Rothery, M. (2006). *Cheating: Definition and consequences*. Unpublished manuscript.

Stefani, L., & Carroll, J. (2001). The LTSN Generic Centre Assessment Series No 10. A briefing on plagiarism, Learning and Teaching Support Network. Retrieved July 26, 2009, from http://www.swap .ac.uk/docs/ltsnbrief10plagiarism.pdf

Talab, R. S. (2000). Copyright, plagiarism, and Internet-based research projects: Three "golden rules." *Tech Trends, 44*(4), 7–9.

Taylor, S. (1998). *Guidelines for constructing and presenting a poster*. Available through Foster-family Based Treatment Association of North America, 1415 Queen Anne Road, Teaneck, NJ 07666.

Thomlison, B., & Jacobs, R. J. (2006). Developing a systematic evidence-based search plan for a client with co-occurring conditions. In A. R. Roberts and K. R. Yeager (Eds.), *Foundations of evidence-based social work practice* (pp. 163–181). New York: Oxford University Press.

Thomlison, B., Jacobs, R., & Becker, J. (2008). Identifying evidence-based practice interventions for co-occurring conditions. In B. Thomlison and K. Corcoran (Eds.), *The evidence-based internship: A field manual for social work and criminal justice students*. New York: Oxford University Press.

Thyer, B. A. (1994). *Successful publishing in scholarly journals*. Thousand Oaks, CA: Sage.

Westerfelt, A., & Dietz, T. J. (1997). *Planning and conducting agency-based research: A workbook for social work students in field placements*. New York: Longman.

Index